Vernon Blackwood

Faith of a People

PABLO GALDÁMEZ

Faith of a People

The Story of a Christian Community
in El Salvador, 1970–1980

*Translated from the Spanish
by Robert R. Barr*

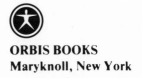

ORBIS BOOKS
Maryknoll, New York

CATHOLIC INSTITUTE FOR
INTERNATIONAL RELATIONS
London, England

DOVE COMMUNICATIONS
Melbourne, Australia

Second Printing, January 1990

First published as *La fe de un pueblo: Historia de una comunidad cristiana en El Salvador (1970–1980),* copyright © 1983 UCA/EDITORES, Universidad Centroamericana José Simeón Cañas, Autopista sur, Jardines de Guadalupe, Apartado Postal (06) 668, San Salvador, El Salvador.
English translation copyright © 1986 by Orbis Books, Maryknoll, NY 10545
All rights reserved
Manufactured in the United States of America

Manuscript Editor: Mary J. Heffron

Library of Congress Cataloging-in-Publication Data

Galdamez, Pablo.
  Faith of a people.

  1. Christian communities—El Salvador.
2. El Salvador—Religious life and customs.   I. Title.
BX2347.72.S2G3513   1986   282′.728423   85–30981
ISBN 0–88344–270–1 (pbk.)

Published in Great Britain by CIIR (Catholic Institute for International Relations), 22 Coleman Fields, London N17AF
CIIR ISBN 0946848 48 3

Published in Australia by Dove Communications, Box 316 Blackburn, Victoria 3130
Dove ISBN 0 85924 443 1

With hope, I dedicate this book

To Bishop Rivera and all of our bishops
        but especially to Archbishop Romero,
        who was murdered on March 24, 1980

To all of our priests and male religious,
        but especially to the ten who have been murdered,
        from Rutilio Grande (March 12, 1977)
        to Marcial Serrano (November 28, 1980)

To all of our religious women,
        but especially to Ita, Maura, Dorothy, Jean,
        who were murdered on December 2, 1980,
        and Silvia,
        who was murdered on January 17, 1981

To all of our seminarians,
        but especially to Otmaro,
        who was murdered on June 25, 1980

To all of the base church communities,
        but especially to all Christians who have
        given their lives for the kingdom of God

To all persons of good will,
        and especially to the priestly people of El Salvador,
        but most especially to all of those
        who have given their lives
        for the liberation of the Salvadoran people,
        for justice,
        and for peace.

You are a chosen race, a royal priesthood, a holy nation, God's own people, that you may declare the wonderful deed of him who called you out of darkness into his marvelous light.

Once you were no people but now you are God's people: once you had not received mercy but now you have received mercy.

Peter 2:9–10

Contents

Foreword

This book is the story of a Christian community of El Salvador. Like so many other Salvadoran communities, this one is small and is a community of the poor. It is located on the outskirts of the capital city, between the fields and the slums, where there is no water system or electricity or school. The people here are poor and deprived, numberless and gloryless. But there is one incredible thing about this poor community. It has a history, and it has made history in El Salvador and in its church. Ten years of that history will be recounted here—the ten decisive years from 1970 to 1980, with their crises, horror, and incalculable pain for the Salvadoran people. Yet these were years of measureless creativity, dedication, and heroism, too. In these ten years, the people and the church of El Salvador emerged from anonymity and uttered a mighty word for the whole world to hear.

This book was written by a priest who lived in that community for ten years. He does not mention his name in his account, so we shall call him Pablo Galdámez—Pablo for Paul the great missionary from abroad; Galdámez because this is a typically Salvadoran name, and our author has truly succeeded in making himself a Salvadoran. He is a European, a "missionary," as he calls himself in the story, with a "mission" like so many other foreign priests. He writes of what he has seen and heard, of what his hands have touched, and of the roads and sidewalks his feet have walked. Doubtless this book is his own story too, as it begins in the days when, all enthusiastic, he came to the community as a young priest; it ends in 1980, when, in great danger, he had to leave the country. ("Better to cry because you're leaving than because you're dead," his friends told him, and they prevailed upon him to leave.) But this is primarily the community's story. It is the community that speaks, that reflects, that doubts, that acts and works, that suffers and is persecuted.

Since this is the history of a community, this book will span a chronological framework broad enough to enable the reader to grasp the story. But it is not a chronicle. It is not interested in dates or details. It is interested in what is deepest in the story, the history, it has to tell. The author seeks to put in words what is profound in daily life. His words, then, will be thoughtful. They are the words of one who has reflected much, for life has given him much on which to reflect. His words will be grateful, too, for they are the words of one who, in the space of ten years, discovered the truth about the poor and about God, the truth about himself, and the truth about history. His words are emotional. They are the words of one who cannot rest content simply with describing what he has seen and heard, without at the same time being seized with, and endeavoring to communicate to the reader, the horror of the evil and the fascination of the good. Finally, his words are a call and a challenge. They are the words of someone screaming, the words of someone who wants to ask others what they are doing for these people.

The author's words have the freshness of truth about them. This is not a book of ideology. It is not even a book of theology. It is simply a book of truth. Truth can easily be clouded over and relativized by ideologies and theologies—as if the purpose of reality were to demonstrate these ideologies or theologies, whereas in actuality, of course, it is the purpose of ideologies and theologies to serve reality, unconditionally. This is why the truth about the poor appears in this book with their names, their lives, their problems, and yes, their shortcomings, their "booze" and their male chauvinism, their lottery and their moneylenders—all the demons that have had to be expelled. But this is why the "other truth" about the poor is so resplendent in these pages— their creativity and solidarity, their dedication and heroism, their faith and hope, their commitment and charity. The most profound truth that this book has to communicate is that the poor have given of their best, and have embarked on an incredible adventure—the adventure of their own liberation and that of a whole people.

All this occurred in stages. This is important to realize in reading this book. The reader might want to start at the end, to learn about the repression and persecution, the popular organizations and the role Christians have played in them, the war and the revolution. But the story did not start there, and neither does the book. Both begin at the beginning with the enormous task of fashioning a people of men and women who are poor, resigned, and disunited, persons who despair, and are alienated. "Build Me a People!" is the title and the story of chapter 1. Next we learn of the little/big exploits of this people, the "Signs of God's Kingdom," as chapter 2 puts it: the little/big miracle of the cooperatives that were formed to help the people break free of the moneylenders, the hygiene courses, the campaign that brought water to the shacks in the gullies. Along with the miracles came the first temptations, yes, and the first desertions. It is hard to stay on the road, especially when the first persecutions flash in the distance!

The more this people became God's people, sent to save the poor, the stronger were the assaults it had to withstand. "Hour of Trial" is the title of chapter 3. The trial was going to be hard, everyone could see that. One had to prepare with faith and courage, but with study, too, with theology and social analyses. There was going to have to be action, and a strong defense of the poor, who were beginning to be massively repressed. "Murder: Not Just in the Movies Now," chapter 3 warns.

Chapter 4 recounts the "Passion, Crucifixion, and Death of the Salvadoran People." This is what El Salvador means to the world. This is the truest of the truths about that country. The basic communities became a full-fledged part of the resplendent church of Archbishop Romero. Then arose the problem of the popular organizations and community participation in them. The community reflected on the prevailing violence, on its causes, on the legitimacy or illegitimacy of a violent response, on encouragement of and solidarity with the persecuted people and their organizations, and on community coresponsibility with Christians living and struggling in the battle zones.

The book ends abruptly on "Good Friday," the Good Friday of the Salvadoran people, the day Archbishop Romero was murdered. End of the book, but not of the life of the community.

And so this book recounts the history of a community. Since it is real history, it is the tale of actual Salvadoran women and men, living, suffering, and reacting to the history of their native land. It is also Christian history, a story lived in the light of the gospel, and with the gospel's commitment and hope. That is why this book examines the story of the community as a journey into the fullness of Jesus. More concretely, we read here of a journey to the priesthood of Jesus. The author uses allegory here. Just as individual priests make the journey to the priesthood step by step, passing traditionally through the stages of porter, exorcist, lector, acolyte, and deacon, and finally arriving at the priesthood—whose "order" includes all of the previous orders—so also the community has had to take these same steps until attaining to its own priesthood with the exercise of all of its powers as the priestly people Scripture tells us it is. First it had to become porter or doorkeeper, and open the doors of the church to the community. Then it had to become exorcist, driving out the demons that beset the progress of the people of God toward the kingdom of God. It had to become lector, or reader, to be able to read and interpret the signs of the times. It had to become acolyte, one who "accompanies," one who makes ready the sacrifice of others. It had to become deacon, one who "serves" those in need. Only then was it finally able to become priest, able to offer Jesus, and itself in Jesus, in sacrifice.

Why the author has chosen the designation of "priestly people" to define his community is easily grasped, if we understand priesthood in terms of the priesthood of Jesus as defined by the Letter to the Hebrews. There is nothing "disincarnate" or ahistorical about this priesthood, nothing purely ritual or symbolic. Rather it is a historical priesthood, a priesthood springing from obedience to the will of God when one's brothers and sisters are concerned, and consummated in the surrender of one's own life. It is not, then, a metaphor or pious description of some kind to call this community a "priestly people." It is deepest reality. It is what this community has been preparing for. This is how its identity, its Salvadoran and Christian identity, is consummated. For this is a community that is giving its life on behalf of its sisters and brothers. This is why too there is such fire of priestly dedication and sacrifice in the accounts in this book of baptism or marriage or confirmation or confession or Eucharist. All is priestly here, and all is real, for all is directed to being able to celebrate one's self-surrender in love.

Jesus' priesthood not only tells of surrender and Good Friday, although these must indeed be, and are so excruciatingly portrayed by the basic communities today. Jesus' priesthood also tells of the hope of resurrection and salvation, which, after all, is what the priestly ministry is ultimately all about. This book is filled with that hope and it ends with that hope: "This crucified people, too, will rise. Indeed, it is rising even as I write these lines." What conviction nourishes that hope? A people that grows in this way, gives of itself in this way, and believes in this way bears within itself the germ of its future resurrection.

This book is a song to a Christian community. It is a song not only to that one particular community, but to a whole people and to a whole church. The community whose life is narrated here is but one among many communities scattered the length and breadth of El Salvador—among the refugees, in the battle zones, in the barrios of the poor in the great cities, and in the countryside. This book is a song to the deed of a people and a church. A little people and a little church, but great in suffering, in fortitude, in hope, in commitment, and in faith. Their most visible manifestations are these communities. Their most shining symbol is Archbishop Romero. What dwells at the heart of these manifestations and these symbols is the faith of a people. Hence our title.

By way of conclusion I should like to add a personal note. For those of us doing theology in El Salvador the reality recounted in books like this one is of supreme importance. Theology has need of "theological occurrences" in the present—historical realities that are God's word and God's people's word. Without these current events, theology will be reduced to a commentary on realities of the past—and so, at times, to texts of the past. All genuine theology lives on the manifestation of God in the present and on the response of God's people in faith, hope, and love in the present. This "present moment of God and God's people" is not reached by theology through insubstantial lucubrations or by study of the already-given. It is reached through realities such as those described in this book.

To put it simply: Theology, too, has to accept what Puebla has to say about the "evangelizing potential of the poor." The poor do not do theology in the technical sense of the word. Nor do their lives and reflections render theology's various functions superfluous. It remains the task of that formal discipline to articulate the present with God's revelation in the past, to relate the present to tradition and the magisterium, to illuminate it by theological reflection and social analysis to foresee the future, to obviate possible dangers, and so on. But all this being said, the fact remains that it is from the poor that theology receives its new eyes to see the gospel and historical reality more correctly, and thus to seize the real theological problems and orientate its response in the proper direction. In a word, the poor, with a radicality and authenticity hardly attainable elsewhere, render present the *res theologica*.

Nor is this *res* ultimately anything other than the gospel of Jesus. It is from within the milieu of the poor, then, that theology can furnish the best explanation of the gospel, seeing itself both challenged to explain that gospel precisely in an evangelical fashion, and enabled to do so: it is in this milieu that theology will be open to the demand of conversion and pierced through with the gladness of the good news.

For all of these reasons, I wish to emphasize that this is the story of the faith of a people, yes, but I also wish to express my gratitude, as a Christian and a theologian, to the people of this faith.

Jon Sobrino

Preface

In April 1981, living in forced exile in Europe, I received a visit from my great friend Lito. First we just talked, a long while. Then we began to meditate on Mary's visit to Elizabeth before the coming of the Savior.

Lito's visit gave me the hope and joy that Elizabeth must have felt when Mary came to see her. Lito compared Europe to the mother of the forerunner. He said that he and I, filled with the living experiences of the Salvadoran people, were a sign, as Mary was to Elizabeth. Latin America, he said, was pregnant, heavy with the Lord. Pregnant with hope, in labor with the new human being. Latin America had good news for Europe.

Lito was so right! I had seen with my own eyes how Christian communities in so many European countries had "leapt for joy" in the womb of their mother church when we came to visit.

After our meditation, we read Mary's song. Together, out loud. The song of a revolution: the Magnificat. And I decided to write this book.

I want to sing a hymn of praise. In oneness with the Christians of the Salvadoran communities, I want to sing a hymn of praise for all that the Lord has done for us. It will be a kind of diary written in a hurry. It will be incomplete, then—simply a collection of impressions from my pastoral experience in El Salvador.

I want to explain, in these pages, the process by which the Salvadoran people—that oppressed, scattered people, prostrate with despair—got up and walked. Started living their Christian faith. And became a priestly people.

Before being ordained a priest, one is ordained porter, exorcist, lector, acolyte, and deacon. That is, before offering sacrifice, one had to open doors, drive out demons, read, and preach and serve. We did all this in our communities, too, priests and people alike. (It didn't make any difference what our official "status" was; we were all becoming "priests in life" in those years.) This is what I want to tell about. The process wasn't systematic. We'd take a couple of steps forward, then we'd fall back a step. It didn't go by dates on the calendar either. What was happening was deeper than any of this. This is what I want to write about. It will be my way of expressing gratitude to God for so much grace—yes, God has been with us, every step of the way—and to my Salvadoran brothers and sisters, whom I love so much.

Faith of a People

CHAPTER ONE

Build Me A People!

Like Working in a Darkroom

The beginning of the Good News about Jesus Christ, the Son of God. It is written in the book of the prophet Isaiah:
> *Look, I am going to send my messenger before you;*
> *he will prepare your way.*
> *A voice cries in the wilderness:*
> *Prepare a way for the Lord,*
> *make his paths straight,*

and so it was that John the Baptist appeared in the wilderness, proclaiming a baptism of repentance for the forgiveness of sins. All Judaea and all the people of Jerusalem made their way to him, and as they were baptized by him in the river Jordan they confessed their sins.

—Mark 1:1–5

Our communities started with people. People looking for salvation. Salvation that went by the name of happiness, friendship, love, justice, life, peace. A great number of people in El Salvador were looking for all this because they didn't have it. They never had it. We, too, were looking, looking for people. We were seeking seekers. We were going to start something new with them!

John the Baptist was sent by God to plunge people into the bath of baptism. God's image in the people around us was covered with

1

dust and dirt. It was unrecognizable. The first thing, then, was to invite the people to wash, to take a bath.

You might say we got the idea that being a missionary was like working for God the Great Photographer, Inc. God had been taking pictures for such a long time, and the film was all here, all stacked up, only it hadn't been developed. Our mission was to develop it, to plunge this film into the developer till out would come the pictures, in living color. Out would come images of the living God.

I still remember the first time I saw José Alberto. He was sitting in his doorway one holiday, hot as a firecracker. Blue eyes, brown hair, with a big streak of white across the top. Now here was a person full of life. He talked with his whole body. He was chock-full of rhythm. He would turn the street into a stage to explain whatever he wanted to tell us. Right from the first, what a terrific negative! And what a picture developed!

Since we were developing negatives, we had to work in the dark. All that discussion with José Alberto and all the others those nights! There in the night, in those San Salvador slum-gullies where the undeveloped negatives were piling up—images of God waiting to be lighted up by the good news—we developed pictures. By candlelight, Leticia would open her gospel and start to understand and so would I. We would understand what Jesus meant about light and darkness. It's when the nights are darkest that you appreciate light the most. And it's in the darkest lives that the light of hope outlines the brightest future.

Because we worked at night, developing pictures and having long, rambling conversations with all those Nicodemuses we were getting to know, we were known as the "bats"—as Silvia found out, when, like a nervous little bat, she started to make night flights to the Tutunichapa slum. The superiors in her convent started to worry. Why did she have to go out so much at night? But this was one you couldn't coop up. She kept getting away. She knew you could only develop pictures in a darkroom. God only knows how many shots she finally developed. (After all, she converted a whole convent into a bats' nest!)

That's how we got started. That's how you always get started—demolishing the dark by sheer patience and light, trying to clean up the messy faces of all those men and women, all those victims of misery and despair.

Opening New Doors, Ringing New Bells

> *This encounter with the poor has enabled us to recover that
> central truth of the gospel with which God's word thrusts us
> toward conversion. The church has good news to announce
> to the poor. People who, in their secular lives, have been
> hearing only bad news, and living worse realities, now are
> listening to the word of Jesus proclaimed through the church:
> "The kingdom of God comes near . . . and happy are you
> poor, because yours is the kingdom of God." And that's good
> news for the rich, too: they must be converted to the poor in
> order to share with them the treasures of the kingdom.*
> —Archbishop Romero, Louvain, Feb. 2, 1980

To become a priest one has to go through a number of steps. The
first ordination used to be that of porter or doorkeeper. The
doorkeeper's job was to open the church doors and ring the bells to
let everybody know the celebration was starting and to invite them
to share the liturgy.

This is not an abandoned tradition. The Salvadoran people, who
became the people of God in the base communities, experienced
this stage. They went through it when I and others—the first
pictures developed in those dark nights—began to gather others
and open doors of hope for them, when hope seemed lost for-
ever.

When Jesus' disciples first started getting acquainted with him
on the banks of the Jordan, they didn't completely understand who
he was, or where they themselves were going to be going now—but
they stayed with him that evening. They answered his invitation.
Almost at once, they became witnesses of what they had "seen"
in Jesus, the new life they felt trembling within them when they
were in his company. And they began to call their friends and
family to come along. They couldn't keep the good news to
themselves. Andrew went to find his brother Peter, Jesus went
and called Philip, Philip went looking for Nathanael. They
called one another. They didn't know yet that as disciples of
the Lamb of God they would be sent out like lambs in the midst
of wolves.

I could write the story of everybody's vocation here—how they were called. Rodolfo, Alberto, Timoteo, Manuel, Mary, Carmen, Isabel, Toño, Rosita, Santiago, Pablo, Tere, Ana, Daisy, Susana, Benjamin, Nacho. . . . Stories full of life, emotion, and gratitude. Stories of men and women who joined hands and walked through the door into the community.

Now we are all part of the history of God's people in El Salvador. This history is not all written yet and we don't know where or how it will end. The one thing we're sure of is that God has decided to write history with us. And of us, the very poorest, God has fashioned a people. This people of God began to come together at the call of the doorkeepers. There has to be somebody to call the others in God's name, somebody to say what's happening, somebody to open the door so that the last—who, for Jesus, are the first—can come into the church, which is the community and not just a building.

This is how our communities began—by calling people to congregate, inviting them to come together. The invitees multiplied and became doorkeepers themselves. Andrew called Peter, Philip called Nathanael.

Demon Booze

They went as far as Capernaum, and as soon as the sabbath came he went to the synagogue and began to teach. And his teachings made a deep impression on them because, unlike the scribes, he taught them with authority.

In their synagogue just then there was a man possessed by an unclean spirit, and it shouted, "What do you want with us, Jesus of Nazareth? Have you come to destroy us? I know who you are: the Holy One of God." But Jesus said sharply, "Be quiet!" Come out of him!" And the unclean spirit threw the man into convulsions and with a loud cry went out of him. The people were so astonished that they started asking each other what it all meant. "Here is a teaching that is new," they said, "and with authority behind it: he gives orders even to unclean spirits and they obey him." And his reputation rapidly spread everywhere, through all the surrounding Galilean counytryside.

—Mark 1:21–28

The first demon that had to be driven out of our people was demon booze, drink. Alcohol had wrecked God's image in so many of these people. They had no control over themselves. They were possessed by uncontrollable forces.

This was the way with Chico. He would spend all day drinking. Every weekend he could be found either in a bar or outside one throwing a fit. He would talk to himself and shout, completely possessed by the spirit of rum, an evil spirit that had destroyed him. He and his wife Maria had had seven children. They lived in a pasteboard shack. Chico belonged to the paramilitary group ORDEN, "Order." His papers saved him from jail. Otherwise he'd have landed there for sure during one of his binges. The loan sharks chased him in one door and out the other trying to get back their cash. But he'd already spent it on booze. And he'd already sold the best things in his house to pay them something. He was at the end of his rope. He'd "hit bottom." And so, in the middle of a binge one night, he decided to kill himself.

He went off and got some rope to hang himself. The evil spirit had overcome him. When he started getting the noose ready to put around his neck, neither his wife nor his children were frightened yet. They were used to his crazy actions. But when Maria saw him actually hanging, she went for the neighbors. They all came running with machetes, and cut the rope. Chico fell to the floor, still alive, shouting, "Lemme alone! I wanta die! Mind your own business! I wanta die!" And he went for his own machete then to go after his neighbors. But they didn't give up, they took his machete away and tied him up. They kept him prisoner for several days, until he finally quieted down. Then they opened the community doors to him, and the doors of Alcoholics Anonymous. Only those neighbors of his, members of a base community, would ever know how many fits the evil spirit, the spirit of booze, had given Chico before finally going out of him and leaving him free.

On the road to the priesthood the second step was ordination as an exorcist. Our communities, too, took this step. We had no theory, no rite. But we clearly saw that we couldn't get to be priests without being exorcists first.

Chico's case surprised people. It pointed down a new road. Evil spirits could be driven out! This good news spread like wildfire to every hovel in the slum. In time Chico became a community doorkeeper. He would invite others to follow the path he'd started on. He'd tell them how demon booze had left him. . . . His shack, still poor but free now, was turned into the "synagogue" where a people would gather looking for freedom.

Hardened drunks were delivered from demon booze, men who had lost their feelings for their wives were freed from their machismo, women who had lost their diginity in prostitution were liberated from the misery that had driven them into the hands of this demon. The people, so many people, who had been under the control of the demon of individualism, began to join hands with their neighbors. Their deliverance was at hand.

A Reading from the Book of Real Life

Our communities are like a tree. In the ground, invisible to the eyes, are the roots, whose tips are at once the strong and the weak point of the tree. They are its strong point because through these thousands and thousands of tips the tree sucks up the sap of the earth. They are its weak point because the ends of the roots are fragile, so fragile. The least shock damages them, bruises them. Without this permanent fragility in the roots, however, the tree cannot rise up out of the ground healthy and strong, cannot replenish itself and keep on living. This fragility must be maintained, even cultivated, certainly not eliminated! The higher the tree, the deeper and broader the root must be. This is what gives the tree its strength. Thus strength appears as the culmination of weakness. In other words, what is strong and powerful is human contact, spontaneity, the risk of events, conversation, personal problems, a whirl of friends, informality, disorganization and seeming inconsistency—in the midst of a people who are poor, weak, and suffering, people marginalized and oppressed, people voiceless and vote-less, people struggling for survival, people with little instruction or study, people with innumerable problems. This is the weak, ever-renewed root of the strength of our great tree which is grown now: our communities.

—Carlos Mesters, *Una Iglesia que nace del pueblo*

It was a great miracle to see a scattered people come together again. We were beginning to be *one* people. Everywhere little groups were forming, becoming communities. The gospel was the book from which the communities learned who they were, and from which they learned the reality of the situation in which they lived.

In my parish, the first group was formed one Sunday at the homily. We were having a dialogue on the gospel and were looking for a path to follow. We were looking for answers. We were even looking for questions. This collective homily annoyed some I remember. One gentleman stood up and said, "Please, don't mix politics and Mass!"

But when Mass was over some of the congregation stayed to talk. And that's when things got started. We had to get together more often, we said. We had to train, we had to learn some answers. We had to learn to "give an account of our hope" (1 Pt 3:15). Suddenly there was the offer of a house to meet in, and I had my first base group.

A friend of Father Chepe's, a person who worked in a co-op, started meeting with some fellow workers of his. A newly married couple found out about our groups and offered their home as the "synagogue." A nun assigned to social work near the parish took charge of another group. On the south side was a slum we hardly knew about. A member of our community who worked in a clinic discovered it and started a little group there. In the slum next to us lived a boy who worked at the university. He started getting people together there. Another group started working twenty kilometers from the parish, directed by a member of our own community. A sister who worked fifty kilometers from the capital got together with a few young people there and started some more communities. The project mushroomed.

So it came about that in the midst of these little groups, so full of problems but alive, we started being lectors. The lectorate used to be third step along the road to the priesthood. We too were lectors, readers, in the Salvadoran slums and ghettos.

With God's word in hand, we tried to find answers to our problems, and we learned where to find the will of God so that we could keep moving ahead. That will was to be found in life, in our conscience, which tells you what's good and what's bad and which shows you're happy when you are. When this conscience, each one's conscience, starts interacting with other people's consciences collectively, in community, when you dialogue with your sisters and brothers, you can read God's will. We also learned to read this will of God in the Bible. One who can read life can easily discover the key to Holy Scripture, with all those living stories of a people on its way to freedom. Another place to read the will of God is in the Christian community. In our group meetings we discovered trails leading to signs of God. And finally, in the poor. They are the best book when it comes to knowing what God wants. We only had to keep asking ourselves, "What are we doing? Does it help the poor or not?" And if it did, we kept it up.

Life itself was giving us the "subjects" to discuss at our meetings. Political life, family and neighborhood life, the life of work or study—we learned to be readers in the community so that the community could be converted into a people able to read the signs of God in the book of history.

Making Ready for a Long Journey

> *On leaving the synagogue, he went with James and John straight to the house of Simon and Andrew. Now Simon's mother-in-law had gone to bed with fever, and he told him about her straightaway. He went to her, took her by the hand and helped her up. And the fever left her and she began to wait on them.*
>
> —Mark 1:29–31

Sometimes I didn't feel like going out and visiting people again, I was tired. But if my friend Chepe was out visiting, it was no use trying to stay home, myself. I had to go out too. And when I came back I felt much better. The "fever" had left me. All those people, all those meetings, had given me back my life. Chepe was a toughie, a real dynamo. Many's the time he "healed" me, took me by the hand and helped me up—made me get up, actually. It's like what Robinson says about this passage from Mark: "Peter's mother-in-law had no choice. Jesus had come. She had to get up. She couldn't stay in bed when Jesus was coming. So the fever *had* to leave her!" I think this is a magnificent explanation. This is such a simple miracle, a miracle that can happen in the midst of ordinary daily life.

And this is what happened in our communities. To grow in awareness, to keep reading new calls in hard reality, to respond to new opportunities, to undiscover the "demons"—all this took effort. It's a long road, and you have to travel it together. You have to take a little bit of everything along with you in your knapsack because the danger is that after the first euphoria, hardship can slap you down.

On the road to the priesthood, after ordination to the lectorate, the candidate is ordained to the ministry of acolyte. The acolyte is the Mass server, the one who carries the bread and wine to the altar, the one who prepares the altar for the sacrifice. The acolyte also carries the candles, the light that shows the way.

We did this too. In those slums, where there were so many limitations, we didn't get up every day in the same mood. We always needed somebody to keep pushing us along the road. Week after week, meetings. Week after week, community building. "But who'll look after the kids?" Or, "What'll we do with Gram?" Or, "I haven't got time right now." There was always some little obstacle we could use as a pretext for inertia.

And so, an "order of acolytes" sprang up in our communities. Some watched the kids during the meetings, others helped members finish their work so they could come on time, still others took chairs or glasses to the poorest hovels so there couldn't be any excuses. And when people were embarrassed to have the meeting in their shack because the roof leaked and the community would get wet, there was still a way to have a meeting. We fixed the neighbor's roof.

This was our "order of acolytes." The acolytes were the ones who made it possible to have the meetings. They straightened life out a bit so that the call could be heard and so that the good news of hope would find the way open. They prepared life's altar so that the community could prepare for the sacrifice God expected from it.

The End of the World

> We face life together,
> Together at break of day,
> Together we're the day's first beam,
> The new morn's gleaming ray.

Together, shoulder to shoulder,
In solid ranks of love,
Together we forge—the new world of peace
That's soon to come from above.

—Community song

El Salvador's priestly people was being born. Without realizing it, we were preparing for the great sacrifice. The doorkeepers called us to a new life. Demons left the hearts of so many people. We read in our meetings, with hope, of the good news. Acolytes started training us to be available to our neighbor. Then we got the inspiration that the great sign of entry into this people, a people that wanted to obey God's will perfectly, should be the sacrament of baptism. We wanted to be born again of water and Spirit.

We celebrated this new baptism in what we called "first level meetings." They lasted two days. It wasn't easy to work up these meetings. You had to find somebody to take care of the kids, you had to get off work. . . . And more than anything else, you had to be persuaded. Some people were afraid. Others said there was no point in going. (A lot of people realized they'd have to leave this meeting more committed. They'd have to put down the bottle. They'd have to stop seeing a lover, or what not.)

But a great number of people came to the first meeting. You'd have thought it was the end of the world! Timid, frightened, they strode forth to meet the unknown. Never before had they left home for more than a day, except for liquor or a lover. Now they were leaving with clear heads, and it was their own wives who fixed them up a little box of things: some clothes, a little hardtack. And all the neighbors were doing the same, off on the adventure together! The kids gave their dads a goodbye kiss. Nothing like this had ever been seen!

Well, it *was* the end of the world. It was the finish of disunity in the neighborhood. And I thought: *"Caramba,* anything's possible!"

That meeting was crucial. And the meetings that followed reinforced the first. The story of El Salvador is a strange one to begin with. And now these denizens of the poorest barrios, considered the dregs of society, the "last," felt called and chosen to start a new story, a new history, a history "from below." For the first time in their lives they had faith in themselves. They understood they had a mission. They knew they weren't alone and that when you have companions, friends, and neighbors all pushing with you, you'll make history. You'll tell a new story.

They went home full of dynamism. Their wives and children were waiting for them. This too was new. When they came back, their wives gave them a smile and their kids gave them a kiss.

New life emerged from that meeting. Those men became doorkeepers, exorcists, readers, acolytes. They were ready for anything. For the first time, we had a permanent, organized pastoral team. The first fruit of this "baptism" was felt in the family. The husband began to support his wife in her tasks, and the wife her husband in his. They realized that the best witness they could give was their own life of family fidelity. These people's mission, the mission of these pioneers of a priestly people, was showing us an important aim for everybody, and stood as a sign of how to achieve it. That aim was the conquest of disunity. Everything was so simple! And yet we felt as if we were seeing the last days of the world.

First Temptations

Then Jesus was led by the Spirit out into the wilderness to be tempted by the devil. He fasted for forty days and forty nights, after which he was very hungry, and the tempter came and said to him, "If you are the Son of God, tell these stones to turn into loaves." But he replied, "Scripture says:

Man does not live on bread alone

but on every word that comes from the mouth of God."

The devil then took him to the holy city and made him stand on the parapet of the Temple. "If you are the Son of God," he said, "throw yourself down; for Scripture says:

He will put you in his angel's charge,

and they will support you on their hands

in case you hurt your foot against a stone."

Jesus said to him, "Scripture also says:

You must not put the Lord your God to the test."

Next, taking him to a very high mountain, the devil showed him all the kingdoms of the world and their splendor. "I will

*give you all these," he said, "if you fall at my feet and worship
me." Then Jesus replied, "Be off, Satan! For Scripture says:
        You must worship the Lord your God,
        and serve him alone."
        Then the devil left him, and angels appeared and looked
after him.*

—Matthew 4:1–11

Not just once, but all his life long, Jesus had to fight temptations. It wasn't just once that temptations appeared in the life of our people either. We had to fight constantly in order to win.

The first temptations were not long in coming. After the meetings, our neophytes would go back to the same hovels, the same poverty, the same wife and the same children, meet with the same neighbors and the same cronies, the same old loafers. *They* felt changed, but reality hadn't changed. The temptations were strong.

"You gotta take it easy, man. Whattaya get outa working, for everybody else? You oughta look out for yourself. Meetings every week! Yer bustin' yer butt for nothin'. Small thanks you'll get! If you've got all that time you oughta pick up a part-time job and make a little extra money. . . . Sure, if you've got time, you can go to all those meetings, but if you haven't. . . . When do you relax? Wanta watch a little TV?"

It's always easier to be comfortable than to serve others. It's easier to swim with the stream and go to the bar after work. It's easier to eat bread than pick your way among the stones.

"What's goin' on with you, fella? Gonna quit yer job and go off to the seminary? Never thought they'd make an altar boy out of you! Henpecked, eh? They're brainwashin' you. . . . that's what. Never takes a nip no more, or a gal neither. Maybe he's gettin' too old to do it no more!"

It was hard to stand up to the neighbors making fun of you day in and day out, especially when your macho, alcoholic, individualist past was still so fresh.

"Hey, gone soft in the head? You go ahead with those stupid 'commitments,' they'll have you in their pocket but good. Look, you wear yourself out for the priests, and the priests don't give a goddam. They're off havin' fun somewheres. They split, and there you are, holdin' the bag. Yeah, high and dry, man."

When you're brought up with temptations like that that are part of the system,where the law is "watch out for number one," and "take what you can get"—well, we had a long way to go to be free from so many temptations. And we learned plenty along the way.

Standing up to Alcoholism and Male Chauvinism

The church has not only taken flesh in the world of the oppressed and given them hope—it has made a firm commitment to their defense.
　　　　　　　　—Archbishop Romero, Louvain, Feb. 2, 1980

Before you get to be a priest, you're a deacon. That is, you're a servant. To support the people of our communities in the following of Jesus, in his discipleship, we had to find the things that would make them capable of keeping faithful to their new commitment. So we created different kinds of deaconship, services suitable for this first stage of our Christian life.

Actually, the meetings every week were the first "deaconing" we did. The meetings disciplined us. That discipline would stand us in good stead one day! It was a small thing, but it put us in control of our own lives.

Where alcoholism was the enemy, our *diakonia* was Alcoholics Anonymous. These groups already existed. They were not a creation of the communities, but we learned to profit from them. Drunks—people who only knew how to have fun with their head stuck in a bottle, in a life of total irresponsibility—had learned in our meetings that they were really sick. Some not only realized this, they were willing to submit to treatment for this disease. So the AA therapy became a true *diakonia,* a great service. In the first place, the AA technique for maintaining sobriety relieved these persons of their physical symptoms. And then, the knowledge that the community needed them sober, that the community had many tasks for them to perform, helped the AA program treat the mental, or psychological, facet of the disease.

The families, too, needed a *diakonia.* Machismo has destroyed families in El Salvador, as in all our Latin American countries. Ever since the first colonization, the male had been the conquistador, the one with all the rights, while women are simply the suffering victims of men's whims. These roles are perpetuated, from generation to generation: the men beget children—for pleasure, to show their masculinity—and the women have to take care of them. For that matter, children are a kind of security for their mothers, since their father never is. While she cares for the children, he has the right to all the adventures he pleases; nothing is too shameless for him. That's how the *machista* structure works.

I remember Margarita. She was six years old when she ran away from home, looking for help from neighbors. Her Papá was beating her Mamá. He was drunk. He had to show who wore the pants in the family. And what became of Margarita in a few years? She ran off with a man, looking for love. Seven out of ten girls and boys run away from home in El Salvador, looking for happiness. Seventy percent of our families are "irregular." In her desperation, Margarita married too young. She didn't discover her mistake until after her first child was born. Fifteen years later her son will repeat the same story—a story the TV soaps like to use to jerk tears from the people that are going through the same thing in real life!

In the face of all this, we thought we had better invent a special *diakonia.* We needed a permanent service to help newlyweds set up housekeeping and start a family, a service that could help heal the wounds of so many families in trouble. A permanent *diakonia.* And so we started our Marriage Encounters.

It was a tremendous challenge. The families have no foundation. Family ties in Latin America are extremely fragile. What holds man and wife together is not love, but stagnation. If they stay together at all, it's for the sake of the children.

I remember Manuel. He'd been married to Francisca thirty-five years. One day he came to tell me that his wife wanted a separation. He begged me to act as go-between, and I went over to hear the other side of the story.

"Father," Francisca said, "it's been thirty-five years of nothing but suffering. Crying every day. I've swallowed everything, I've put up with everything. For the kids, cause I didn't want them to have a stepfather. Now the kids are grown up and married, and my husband keeps on drinking. He's a good-for-nothing. I've done my duty. I've talked to the kids about it, and they told me I've suffered enough. My way of the cross is over."

I listened to everything she had to tell me. There wasn't much I could say. She was one hundred percent right. In thirty-five years of married life she had never known love. She had just put up with everything for her children. Milk money had to come from somewhere. There had to be tortillas and beans. So she'd held out somehow. What can you tell someone like that?

One day I asked Marta why each of her children had a different papá. (We were good friends, so I could ask that.)

"Look, Father, I had the first when I was a kid. This boy, I fell in love with him, he knocked me up, we screwed. It lasted six months. He had this other woman, and the fights started. He took off, and there I was, pregnant . . . It's been that way all my life. Every man lied to me. They're all the same, Father."

What could we say to Marta? She had never known love. She was not a bad woman. It was just that she had suffered so much, and there was no way out of the suffering.

The deaconship of the Marriage Encounters—where we analyzed each case dispassionately and proposed solutions as a group—put us on the right road. It was with Marta, Francisca, and all the other men and women who had never known love, that we were going to have to fashion a priestly people in El Salvador.

Rescuing the Sacrament of Marriage

Love is always patient and kind; it is never jealous; love is never boastful or conceited; it is never rude or selfish; it does not take offense, and is not resentful. Love takes no pleasure in other people's sins but delights in the truth; it is always ready to excuse, to trust, to hope, and to endure whatever comes.

—1 Corinthians 13:4–7

The Encounters made our people want to be responsible for their lives. And since life begins at home, for the first time questions about the sacrament of marriage came up. People were discovering the feeling of love, and so they were starting to look at their union with new eyes. And strangely, they wanted to "get married" all over again, "for real." They didn't ask to go to church for a wedding.

They sought out the community. They wanted to promise fidelity in the midst of the community.

This new situation set our communities thinking. Thinking a lot. When you get right down to it, the way a person acts who gets married in church and one who just "screws" isn't outwardly any different. The sacrament is completely invisible. In fact, it seemed to us that the only people who got married in church were the rich, the ones with cash.

The sacrament of marriage in El Salvador, it would seem, is more like a anti-sacrament. In many cases it is nothing but a class-bound ritual, since only those with money can receive it. The social pressure is so great that the poor don't dare ask to be married in church. They associate that with new clothes, extra expenses, flowers on the altar, a rented limo, a big dinner, music, a rug on the floor, and all the rest of it. If there's no money to pay for all this, it looks like a third-class wedding, and the poorest of the poor feel humiliated. In order to be married by the church, peasants often have their marriages blessed by a priest giving a mission, several couples at a time.

Sometimes, however, a man is forced to accept a marriage blessed by the church. To get his bride, he had to agree to what the girl's mamá says. It's completely against his will. So a marriage blessed by the church doesn't mean a more secure marriage. On the contrary, it often makes for an even more painful drama.

We analyzed all this in community. Together we examined the case of Medardo. Twenty years before, Medardo had gotten married in church, as the girl's parents had demanded. It was over in less than six months. Afterwards, he had five children with another woman. Now he wanted to have this marriage blessed by the church, because now he could see what this sacrament was. What could we tell Medardo? How could we make a connection between the rigid law of the church on this point and people's real lives—such different lives, lives so hard to judge by law alone? What could we tell people who told us, "No, we're not gettin' married in church. We wanta be happy. It's the devil to pay when you get married in church. We'll just stay the way we are"?

From all of these problems and anxieties, we were discovering all over again what marriage means in the church community. Couples were finding that for their work to be credible they had to declare their fidelity before the community. They were discovering that they were not only wife and husband, they were support for one another in the Christian task. And they wanted to be happy. What was soon to be loyalty to the people to the death, began by loyalty and fidelity in married life.

And so we started celebrating marriages. Not everybody got married at the same time. Some needed a lot more time to prepare, to straighten out a whole series of situations. Others were ready more quickly. Those first weddings were unforgettable fiestas. The whole community was there, including the couples' children. Nobody was shocked. For the kids, it was an honor to be there to hear their mom and dad promise mutual love. And the community presence was a community commitment to defend that love always. Those fiestas were also the sign of God's fidelity, a sign of God's commitment to the poor, who, after all, are God's people. That was really a sacrament.

"These People Aren't Catholics, They're Subversives!"

Then some of the Pharisees said, "This man cannot be from God: he does not keep the sabbath." Others said, "How could a sinner produce signs like this?" And there was disagreement among them. . . .

So the Jews again sent for the man and said to him, "Give glory to God! For our part, we know that this man is a sinner." The man answered, "I don't know if he is a sinner; I only know that I was blind and now I can see." They said to him, "What did he do to you? How did he open your eyes?" He replied, "I have told you once and you wouldn't listen. Why do you want to hear it all again? Do you want to become his disciples too?" At this they hurled abuse at him. . . .
                                                                —John 9:16, 24–28

About this time, a number of priests began lodging complaints against us. "These 'base communities' are sowing division in the church. They disregard tradition. They have no respect for the saints. What sort of new sect are they, anyway?" Others said, "But the people have changed. They're off their booze, they get married in the church. It's a miracle!" And there was disagreement among them.

The first persecutions we suffered came from men of the church, from priests, all acting very piously. This was natural, of course. Until now, the faith of our people had been nothing but empty tradition. Now things had changed. Now our people's life had changed, right to the roots. And this put a lot of official persons on the spot! Our people really didn't much care about the patronal feast days any more. There was certainly nothing genuinely religious about these "bashes." The liquor manufacturers would get rich, religious sentimentalism would run wild, and the whole thing would wind up in booze and promiscuity. For the first time, questions came up about certain "traffickers in the faith." Why was there so much talk about holy water and novenas, and so little about commitment to neighbor and social change?

Alfonso told us how he would come home at night "half-looped" and see the little candle his wife had burning in front of the statue of Saint Michael to petition that Alfonso would stop boozing and settle down. Well, one night Alfonso came home and just pitched the candle out the window. He'd just learned in our meetings that a drunk doesn't "settle down" because somebody lights a candle. He'd decided to go to Alcoholics Anonymous for help. What good was babbling all these long prayers, he said, when *he* was the one who had to do something about it?

People were waking up. As they opened their eyes, they started being very hard on the religion they'd been taught. So when they heard certain priests criticizing them, they didn't just sit there and keep quiet. They answered back, like the person blind from birth in the Gospel of John. "Look, I don't know whether these communities are Christ's or what, but I know one thing: Before, I was blind. Now I see. Funny you with all your knowledge about God don't know what these communities are, because that's where we've been healed!"

Then the powers-that-be started their attacks. When people are converted they become dangerous. They start critically analyzing what's going on in their country. So the authorities went on the offensive. "They're fooling the people," "They're using religion to get people to rebel against the government. They're Communists in sheep's clothing. They're subversives!"

Then we got a letter from the Ministry of the Interior, ordering us priests to report there. They had received a formal accusation. We'd been denounced as subversives. According to the accusation we were trying to get the students and the peasants to rise up against the government. The whole thing was false. In fact, we weren't even working with students or peasants at that time. The saddest thing, though, was to learn that the denunciation had been signed by four priests belonging to the paramilitary organization ORDEN. At the Ministry we had to promise to carry on our pastoral work "within the bounds of the Constitution of El Salvador and the teaching of the church."

That's all we'd been doing anyway. But of course any consciousness-raising, any conscientization of the poor, even at this individual and family level, always had considerable social consequences. Then the papers' attacks on our communities, the big headlines—this was even more conscientizing for everybody! For the first time we understood that we would run into persecution at every turn along the road we had taken. I remember how encouraged we were in those first conflicts by this passage from the Letter to the Hebrews:

> Only a little while now, a very little while,
> and the one that is coming will have come; he will
>   not delay.
> The righteous man will live by faith,
> but if he draws back, my soul will take no pleasure
>   in him.

You and I are not the sort of people who *draw back,* and are lost by it; we are the sort who keep faithful until our souls are saved. [Heb. 10:37–39]

And so, from the very beginning we could see that right in the midst of the Salvadoran people a priestly people had been born, a people that would be able, as the prayer for the ordination of a priest puts it, to "dis-cover" the mystery of the death of our Lord Jesus Christ.

The first step had been taken. Like Abraham, our communities had received the call to form a people, a sign of God's future, a tool for building a new world. We didn't know where we were

going, who our "descendants" would be, or in what God's bless-
ing would consist. With the same doubts Abraham had, we
started off down the road. The people had been built now, a
unified people of God.

CHAPTER TWO

Signs of God's Kingdom

Lucky the Poor: For That's What God Wants Them to Stop Being!

> *Awakening to these realities and feeling their impact, far from leading us away from our faith, has sent us back to the world of the poor as our rightful place—has moved us, as a first, basic step, to take flesh in the world of the poor. This is where we have found the actual faces of the poor that we hear about in Puebla. Here we have found landless peasants, without steady jobs, without water or lights in their hovels, without medical services when the mothers give birth, and without schools when the children begin to grow up. . . . Here we have found people living in slums that are more miserable than you can possibly imagine.*
> —Archbishop Romero, Louvain, Feb. 1, 1980

Now we were a people. We were like a big family. We were friends. The community meetings bound us closer and closer together. The doors were open. We said hello to one another, we went to one another's houses. For the first time, this scattered people was united. Gone were fear and embarrassment. We shared everything, a cup of coffee, a glass of water—and the quest. We'd learned to search out the solution to our problems together. There had been so many who had had no time to reflect on them and try to find a remedy.

Carlitos taught us that sickness wasn't the result of irresponsibility. Sickness came from unsanitary conditions. And unsanitary conditions were the result of poverty. We also discovered that children's sicknesses were almost always due to malnutrition. And we learned that children weren't malnourished because their mothers were irresponsible. They were malnourished because their mothers were poor.

Carlitos was five years old. He had no toilet in his house, so he had to go to the bathroom a few yards outside his little shack. One night his mother heard him screaming. His intestine had come out. We took him to the hospital in a taxi. I'd never seen this. What could be the matter? The diagnosis: "Malnutrition, second degree." What to do for him? "Tell his mamá to give him an egg a day and a little piece of meat. And milk, too." Berta didn't even have the money for the taxi we took to the hospital! She had five more children, and her husband was a garbage collector.

Not long after, there was Sandra. I went to her shack to pay her a visit and found her crying.

"He's dying! My Benjamin is dying!"

The little boy looked very ill indeed. At the doctor's it was the same story: malnutrition. The doctor asked Sandra how many children she had.

"Seven," she replied.

You should have heard the doctor scold her. "Sandra, we're people, not animals. It's your fault this boy is sick. The other children are sick too, I'm sure!"

This was too much for Sandra. Sobbing, she said to the doctor, "They always say the same thing, I've got too many kids! Nobody ever asks me how much my husband makes! And you, how many kids do you have? How much do you make? I bet *you* make ends meet!"

The doctor was silent. He gave her some medicine—no charge—and told her he'd come to see the other children the next day—no charge.

Most Salvadorans live like this. To be healthy is a privilege. To have medicine or even access to a doctor is a luxury. When it's a matter of life and death, the poor have no recourse other than the loan shark. Loan sharks charge ten to twenty percent interest—per day. But there's no other way out. The victims are sick persons, bereaved families, abandoned wives, and the disabled. What can you do about something like this?

What can you do about a girl who becomes a prostitute to save her little brother's life? Or the children who never set foot in school because there's no school in the barrio, or because there's no money to buy a pair of pants to wear to school, or because they have to stay home with their little brothers and sisters while their mamás are minding their stalls in the marketplace?

We found out that the poor pay more for light than do people who have electricity. The poor use candles. And they use the candles only as absolutely necessary, just enough to see to get around in the dark without bumping into things. It's hard to get up much enthusiasm for reading by candlelight, much less for studying. Four candles a night makes 120 candles a month, and that's four times as expensive as two lights burning all night long.

The same goes for water. In the slums you have to buy your water. There's no piped water. You need ten jugs a day to wash your clothes, to cook, and for everybody to have a bath. And then many women make their living by taking in washing. The ten extra jugfuls of water they buy cost four times as much as it would if they had a water system.

This is the way it is with everything. The poverty of the Salvadoran people is unimaginable. And it was among them that God was choosing a people! To believe this took an act of faith. This is the way I lived, this is the way we all lived—like the shepherds around Bethlehem, who found in the poorest child there the messiah.

Many was the time we found the same thing as the shepherds. One of us would find it, and invite the others to draw near to this poverty, share it, and see God in it. One time it would be Rosita: "Hey, I found a new slum, over that way kinda. We have to get over there!" Another time it was Maria: "You know, behind those buildings are thousands of shacks? Let's get going!"

It was no fun going to a new slum. The people looked at us suspiciously. The dogs snarled threateningly. But, as at the world's first Christmas, when the Savior was born in misery, so it was among these wretched women and men that there was born and grew the people of God in El Salvador.

Hour of the Miraculous Sign

*A youth, who wished to attain to the highest degree of human
knowledge, went for advice to an experienced teacher, who
had had little formal training but was very wise.*

"Sir," asked the youth, "what is the highest knowledge?"

"To know the limits of knowledge," the other replied.

*"Who can teach me that? Where can I find the school that
will teach me that?"*

*"That school is the people themselves," replied the teacher.
"And its teachers are people who have no learning."*

*And so off went the youth to register in the school of the
people, and become the pupil of those who know nothing.*

      —Carlos Mesters, *Seis dias nos porões da humanidade*

Now more than ever, we were called on to find solutions to so
many life-and-death problems. We were called on to exercise the
sacred function of doorkeeper: ringing bells and opening doors.
And so we did.

When a people have stopped blaming their misfortunes on something outside themselves, and start organizing to fight the causes of
their own wretchedness, the good news of Jesus has dawned on
their horizon.

We knew Berta's little boy needed an egg and a piece of meat
every day if he was to get well. It was pretty much the same thing
with Rosita's son. But there were lots of Bertas, and lots of Rositas,
with undernourished children. So we investigate the problem in depth and soon organized the first Caritas program in our
communities to provide nutritional assistance to children and
mothers-to-be. It was a "sign."

Berta, who did not know how to read or write, came to the
community personally to thank us for saving her little boy's life and
to tell us the story of her poverty. Testimonies like hers were
multiplying. Our community meetings turned into schools of life,
schools where we learned how to live—schools of reflection on
reality, workshops where, like a guild of artisans, we tried to help
one another.

Pedro was a great lesson to us all. He was out of work, and he
was a good carpenter. The community found steady work for him.

It was far from home, though, and he was going to have to find lodging in another city. The evening before he was to start I went to see him.

"You know what?" he began. "I'm not going to be able to take that new job. I've started a little piece of work for a friend of mine. I can't just quit in the middle of it. He helped me when *I* needed it, and I can't back down on my promise."

I argued with him. I told him, look here, he had a chance to have a steady job and security. I told him he should think about his wife and kids.

"Right, Padre, I'm very grateful to the community. But a pal is a pal, and I promised. You see. . . ."

I had nothing to say. I couldn't appreciate his line of reasoning. I didn't understand. I began to think Pedro was just a big old softie, and would rather just wander around here with nothing to do. But I was judging him rashly. And when I looked him in the eye, I could see that there was some other reason.

And the reason was this. Pedro was a freelancer. Every two or three days he would finish a little job and some grocery money would come in. So life was bearable. Nobody starved. But what would happen if he took a new job far from home? He would have to go off and work for a month before getting paid. And how would he and his family eat in the meantime? There he would be, far away, where nobody knew him and nobody would give him credit. Where would he sleep? He didn't even have a hammock to take along. But the worst thing was that his wife and kids only had a three days' supply of groceries. All in all, he'd rather keep looking for small jobs and try to make it one day at a time.

When he'd finished, I felt guilty for thinking unkindly of him. I had never realized that for a poor person it's even hard to take a better job!

From the emergency fund we'd gotten together, though, I managed to get a hammock, and groceries for the family for the first month. Now Pedro could go off and work as a full-time carpenter. It was another "sign."

Another sign: the courses in hygiene we started for the women of the barrio. The little shacks looked cleaner now. Soon there were more signs. Some of the women got an old sewing machine and opened a little tailor shop. We helped them buy more machines, and the enterprise grew into a veritable sewing college!

Antonio, a member of our community, a medical student, began seeing people in the barrio. Nursing courses were started, and some of the girls and young women learned how to give shots and administer certain medicines. From the old women they learned some natural remedies with plants. All of these things were miraculous signs. It was as if winter had passed now, and the rains were making the grass and flowers spring up everywhere. Everyone wanted to contribute something to make life better.

The teachers in our communities started organizing literacy courses. We began to build a little school, since the slum didn't have a single one. Every night we would mix cement, lay bricks, and so on. Everybody helped, men, women, and children. I remember Nacho. Nacho had never been to a meeting; he was too busy drinking. When he saw his neighbors doing construction work he felt "called." Nacho was a bricklayer. He knew everything there was to know about it, and he pitched right in. And so his alcoholism ran smack into the walls of a school! When we were finished we named him Builder of the Year, and toasted him with lemonade!

We even started a squeegee shop. We got hold of some rubber, and Julio took over the management of the "firm." Julio was a good carpenter, and didn't have any trouble making the handles and fittings. I still remember the day we walked out of the shop with dozens of squeegees on our shoulders to sell! A short while later, two soldering shops were in operation.

Miracle of the "Market Place Women"

Now there was a woman who had suffered from a hemorrhage for twelve years; after long and painful treatment under various doctors, she had spent all she had without being any the better for it, in fact, she was getting worse. She had heard about Jesus, and she came up behind him through the crowd and touched his cloak. "If I can touch even his clothes," she had told herself, "I shall be well again." And the source of the bleeding dried up instantly, and she felt in herself that she was cured of her complaint. Immediately aware that power had gone out from him, Jesus turned around in the crowd and said, "Who touched my clothes?"

His disciples said to him, "You see how the crowd is pressing around you and yet you say, "Who touched me?" But he continued to look all around to see who had done it. Then the woman came forward, frightened and trembling because she knew what had happened to her, and she fell at his feet and told him the whole truth. "My daughter," he said, "your faith has restored you to health; go in peace and be free from your complaint."

—Mark 5:25–34

In early June, the "marketplace women" came to see me. They wanted me to celebrate a Mass in honor of the Sacred Heart of Jesus in the marketplace. The devotion to the Sacred Heart is very popular in the Salvadoran marketplaces. The "marketplace women" have made him their Patron and Protector.

These women are an institution in El Salvador. Many are single, abandoned by their husbands. They are very poor, but their courage in the face of difficulties is proverbial. They are dauntless.

Often they get involved with the usury mechanism, the loan sharks. They borrow a little money in the evening. Then the next morning they buy fruit or vegetables. At noon, along comes the moneylender for the interest—twenty percent. Sometimes they pay part of the capital too. On a one hundred colon loan, then, the shark will get ten colons interest the first day plus ten of the capital, then get the same payment for ten days, thus netting one hundred colons' interest. And the capital is all back. That's twenty percent interest per day, since the capital isn't out the whole ten days. The situation is extremely rough, and there seems to be no way out of it. The economic system in which the "marketplace women" survive—barely—has very strong roots.

I agreed to celebrate the Feast of the Sacred Heart with them. I told the community about the case, and we all thought it would be very hard to do anything about the situation of injustice these persons were living in. It was an old, old "illness," and would be very hard to heal. But these were persons of faith. They wanted to "touch Jesus," it seemed to me, like the woman with the hemorrhage in Mark. I was only concerned about their notion that the Sacred Heart was going to reward them with a winning lottery ticket or something! And so their request was a challenge to our communities: we had been healed of so many maladies—now we ought to heal these other persons. The celebration in the market-place really ought to be a liberating one. But how?

I came for Mass on the appointed day. A number of the members of the communities and I went to the little square in the middle of the market. A life-sized statue of the Sacred Heart stood there, all decorated with flowers and streamers. The light from the candles all but outshone the noonday sun. The altar was a little wooden table that wobbled and teetered. On it was a piece of coarse white cotton cloth and a smaller statue of the Sacred Heart. That one belonged to the moneylender. She was right there, somewhere in the crowd. Some of the women thanked God that morning for the profit the moneylender had received! Kids were running around everywhere, and lots of dogs. Under the altar table were bottles of water for me to bless. (The women planned to take this "holy medicine" home with them.) One "market woman," over in a corner, was burning incense. Most wore black shawls. Those who didn't have shawls were shielding themselves from the sun with the front page of the paper (headline: "Milk Prices Up").

The whole scenario annoyed me. We had the idea that we were going to proclaim the good news of liberation here! We were going to "heal" these persons here! I started Mass. The women all sang the music and made the responses. In the homily I opened a dialogue with them—on their love for one another, on the big problems they had—and soon we were talking about the biggest thing that bound them together: no money to send the kids to school, to take them to the hospital, or even to feed them three meals a day.

And up came the subject of the moneylenders. Some of the women expressed gratitude for their services, saying it made it possible for them to survive. Others were silent. Then, timidly, somebody said they only made things worse. There was a moment of confusion. Majestic on his makeshift pedestal, the Sacred Heart of Jesus presided over this decisive moment of "conscientization" when the poor had the floor, when the poor could speak out. Then one of the women shouted out, "The interest sure is high!" Others seconded her, then quickly covered their faces with their shawls, reciting prayers, as if asking forgiveness for their rebelliousness. That was when the moneylender left in a huff.

Then there was fear. Some of the women realized they'd put their foot in it, that their business was done for if they didn't have the loan shark's help. The fear grew. And then, in the midst of the anguish, God's light shone. Couldn't they get together and form a co-op? Wouldn't this be the best way to honor the Sacred Heart of Jesus? One woman said: "They've got this some places. This friend tol' me. And they're doin' fine—better than with the money-lenders that're on *our* necks!"

The miracle had happened. In that moment, the hemorrhage stopped. The illness dried up. The marketplace women felt healing.

At the consecration, there were skyrockets in honor of the Sacred Heart. After what had happened, their sharp reports were like signs of hope launched toward the future. When the celebration was over, the women stayed to touch the mantle of the big statue of the Sacred Heart. I too had "touched" him. We had all seen the miracle. The next day the women met with our community to start a new co-op.

We were sure the moneylender would pressure the women now. We had to make sure we had enough in our emergency fund, we had to get in contact with people who knew more about co-ops than we did, and so on. All kinds of things were happening at once. But the next day the new co-op was on its feet, thanks to money collected from the community. From then on, two new moneylenders came to the marketplace every day—Maritza and Mery, the co-op lenders. They carried their account books with all the data, and they took the money the market women had gotten together. Gradually confidence grew, and with it the number of women in the co-op. Requests for loans were outstripping our meager resources. But we couldn't let these women down.

One year, at the beginning of Lent, we had some trouble. We were short of money. So we asked for a day of fasting in the community to help the market women's co-op. I'll always remember Santiago and the Easter collection. "We saved ten centavos a day," he said. "Here it is." Four colons. Santiago lived in a shack, and actually he and his family had "fasted" all their lives. They had always suffered from hunger. I asked him how he'd managed to get that much together. He told us he'd simply skipped breakfast all during Lent. Those ten centavos a day could have been a hard biscuit and some juice. But he'd saved it to help the women. I thought of those four colons as being like the five loaves and two fishes that Jesus had multiplied in Galilee. That's what happened to these colons. That collection taken up from the poorest of the poor saved the co-op. It was a miracle, and we were all witnesses.

The Daily Miracle: Unity Is Strength

> *The real world of the poor, too, teaches us what Christian hope is all about. The church preaches a new heaven and a new earth. The church also knows that no socio-political configuration can substitute for the final plenitude of what God plans for us. But the church has learned that this transcendent hope must be maintained, kept up, with the signs of historical hope, however simple these signs may seem. They may be like the ones Third Isaiah announces: "They will build houses and inhabit them, plant vineyards and eat their fruit" [Is 65:21]. That there is authentic Christian hope in this—that this is not what some call "reducing" Christian hope to the temporal, the "human"—we see from daily contact with those who have no houses or vineyards, those who build houses for others, and those who sow where others will reap.*
>
> —Archbishop Romero, Louvain, Feb. 2, 1980

At times like these we felt strong. This was because we were united. We were constantly experiencing the "miraculous strength" of our oneness.

Sometimes the subject of electric lighting came up at our meetings. We had to burn so many candles! We appointed a committee to try to get electric lights for the slum. We went to the light company, and they promised to "study the matter." Somebody came up with the idea of going to the papers just in case the company was thinking of filing our application away somewhere and forgetting about it. So we wrote a long letter to the newspapers. It was a shrewd letter—we thanked the company for the attention they had given our request. That did the trick. Shortly after, electricity came to the pasteboard shacks. You could have seen us late in the evenings putting up light poles.

The same thing happened in another slum with drinking water. A group there invited the mayor to come and see the situation with his own eyes. We had photographers there, and they snapped the distinguished gentleman's picture while he was speaking. Now he was compromised, and drinking water came to this slum for the first time.

Elsewhere the water problem turned out to be more difficult. The only way, it seemed, to get water was to lay a main on somebody else's land. And besides, we were afraid our own landowner might take advantage of the situation by waiting until the water main was in and then evicting our community and renting to people who would be willing to pay more.

This set us to thinking about a housing co-op. Some of us started collecting money, others went looking for a good spot to build. Provisional officers were named. At one point we thought we had found a place only to learn that a new street was going to be put right through the tract we had in mind. So we kept on looking. We found another tract. The trouble with this one was that it was so far from town. Chelo summed it up: "Sure, Father," he said, "it's nice and cheap, but it's so far away that we'll have to pay four times as much on the bus—and then the women who take in washing or sell tortillas in the urban districts, what are they going to do? No, it won't work."

As I listened to Chelo gnash his teeth with frustration—because the tract of land was a good one but "wouldn't work"—I understood why San Salvador is ringed with slums, shacks piled one on top of another with such horrible living conditions. These are all people who have come from the interior looking for work. The coffee harvest only lasts two months a year. The same goes for cotton and sugar. What about the rest of the year—all those months of battling hunger and sickness? So the people come to the capital to work on construction gangs or whatever they can find. The first few days they live with friends in the pasteboard shacks and sleep on the floor. Then they set up their own hovels, small and dirty, next to the open sewers that flow down from the rich neighborhoods and make these slums even more repulsive and unhealthy. But at least these people are in the city now, where they can grab whatever job opportunity might come along. Unemployment in El Salvador is an endemic plague.

We had to stick together, then, and find some decent piece of property where we could start our housing co-op. We found one, only we needed a huge pile of cash to buy it. We discovered that a developer wanted to buy the same tract, and so we were at a disadvantage. We lost our chance again. The rich had beaten us.

After so many tries, we learned that we had to stick together. Now only a "miracle" could save us. I knew that there might be some "wise king," like one of the magi, in my own country who would offer us treasure if we asked. I decided to give it a go. I wrote a letter in the name of our co-op and in two months we had the money. We could start looking for property again.

The person who found the property we eventually bought came running. In his hand he held a lovely guaya apple he'd found growing there. I'll never forget his eyes. They said, "This is a land flowing with milk and honey!"

The landlord was ninety years old, and it took some talking, but we finally persuaded him to sell us the land. Then we bought another little strip from a lawyer so that we could have access to the road. The "magi" gave us the money for all this. We started building. Little did I know, as the houses started to rise from the earth, that this community would send so many "missionaries" to other places to proclaim to their sisters and brothers who were still asleep, still disunited, the miracles that happen when the poor unite.

Seven Demons

> "When an unlean spirit goes out of a man it wanders through waterless country looking for a place to rest, and not finding one it says, 'I will go back to the home I came from.' But on arrival, finding it swept and tidied, it then goes off and brings seven other spirits more wicked than itself, and they go in and set up house there, so that the man ends up by being worse than he was before."
>
> —Luke 11:24–26

Some demons were gone now, but others had taken their place. Our community had made increasingly serious commitments now, and demons don't like that. These were the sort of demons that keep you from being brothers and sisters to one another. The demons of individualism and selfishness are the strongest of all, stronger even than demon alcohol. Sometimes they come in disguise and are hard to unmask. Yes, in this stage of our growth we still expelled demons, performing the tough priestly duty of exorcism.

There was Andrés. He was the most active of any of us when it came to seeing to it that the parish had a school. Every day he devoted his time to the project. He was always in the front lines of every campaign. He demonstrated so much responsibility that he was appointed treasurer. Then temptation got the better of him. He ran off with the money and never came back.

There was Ana, who lived on the second floor. The water we had petitioned for had gotten only as far as her floor. Nobody had any on the floors above. We were going around getting signatures to have the water piped all the way up. And Ana wouldn't sign. "I've got my water, why should I worry about anybody else?" (Like Cain: "Am I my brother's keeper?")

The first president of the housing co-op once had a personal problem with another member. Since he was the president, he thought revenge would be easy. He started spreading the story that his "enemy" owned lots of property, and things like that. Then his "enemy" accused him of forging signatures. The problem grew. It caused a great deal of division in the community, and helped nobody. The president, his pride wounded, resigned his office, left the co-op, and threatened to denounce us as Communists.

One day Cristina came to tell us her husband had left her. She didn't know how she would make it with three children. Our savings and loan co-op suggested she set up a lunch stand. She could make tortillas, fill them with cheese or beans, and sell them. We would get her everything she needed: corn, beans, cheese, cracklings, a jug for water, a frying plate, and a bit of kindling. It wouldn't be a big investment for us, and she would be able to make a living right away. We found her a good spot near the bus stop. We only needed somebody to help her get started, so she could learn to make change, since she didn't know arithmetic. Several girls from the upper primary grades volunteered. But when their mamás found *that* out! "What? My daughter, that woman's servant girl? That's her problem, my daughter isn't anybody's peon!" And the girls were forbidden to help Cristina. Their mothers were possessed by the demon of selfishness.

Other members of our housing co-op, too, were in the power of "seven demons." They were happy with their lodging until they discovered that they had the lowest-cost housing in the whole city. Then it occurred to them to sell it for twice the price. Selfishness had entered their hearts, and was stronger than the ties that had bound them to the community all these years.

Sometimes these demons were impossible for us to drive out. But sometimes we were tougher than they were. I remember Hilda. The only thing she had on her mind was going to college. She studied at night till she had her high school diploma. She told me one day that she was going to study business administration. "My friends tell me it's a good career, where I can make plenty of money." I pointed out that there were all these poor people who didn't have a lawyer to defend them, and explained how companies would fire them without compensation.

"There's nobody to watch out for them, Hilda. You'd like to do something for them, wouldn't you? So why not study something that would help them a whole lot?"

I remember how her eyes shone. "Okay! I'll study law for them!" Now she was going to study not for herself, but for others. The demon of selfishness, the seven demons of individualism, left her heart that moment. Thank God our community had the grace of exorcism!

Learning to "Read"

It is important to arouse the people, but the "arouser" must keep aware of the relative value of the arousing. It is not the arouser who commands time and history. On the contrary, it is the arouser who is commanded by history. It is history that brings the time around to the moment before dawn. And this is what makes it possible for the instigator, the arouser, to get something done. It is the river that carries the boat, not the boat the river. It is the history of our people, the history we call secular or profane, that sweeps the bark of salvation history along, and permits salvation to blossom in the con-sciousness today of our people. It is the "profane" history of the people that marks the kairos—*the hour, the moment determined by God. It is not we who make that determination. Our task is to be attentive, to read the signs of the "hour of God" in the history of our people, to bear testimony to it by a lively response and devoted acceptance, and to proclaim it to others as the good news.*

—Carlos Mesters, *Una Iglesia que nace del pueblo*

How many extra meetings we had to hold in those days! There were so many things to organize, and quickly. There were so many problems to solve, so many signs to perform, so many demons to expel. We knew we had to proclaim the kingdom of God, and we had to learn to read the signs of God's coming into people's lives. We learned to do this by staying faithful to our prayer. Prayer is nothing but listening to the Lord acting in history. Prayer is listening to God's word in our conscience, in Holy Scripture, in the community, and in the poor. Praying was the most important thing the community leaders did. They had to pray faithfully so as to be able gradually to learn to read, so as to be able to carry out the priestly task of lector, reader.

A few gains, a few "miracles," and some people's euphoria knew no bounds. It was just as when Jesus had multiplied the loaves: for some, Jesus was now the one to follow all right—but only because he ran a cut-rate bakery, that was all. The same thing happened to some of us. The day when our little school, smack in the middle of the slum, was finished, some people could only see all those bricks that had been laid. Once the housing co-op was in full swing, there were people who could only see the chance for low-cost housing. But this shouldn't have been enough. The little school, the co-op— these things ought to have created community for a further purpose, for greater commitments.

So this was a challenge. The community readers had the mission of reading these signs out loud for everybody to hear. Their job was to drag us out of our illiteracy.

One day we were reflecting on how God had created human beings in the divine image—heads high, straight and tall, ready to meet their sister and brother. One woman said, "But some of them are more like cattle. They walk on all fours, they look at the ground. They're nearsighted and selfish. They forget about everybody else. Not a thought about God. Cattle they are."

Jesus, too, knew this sorrow. He wasn't a magician flaunting his healing powers. He wasn't a baker going around passing out free bread. His signs proclaimed the kingdom of God. They were invitations to conversion. They were calls to prepare for a new age. His signs were a denunciation of the world the way it was, selfish and idolatrous, the old world. Jesus was issuing an invitation to the new world, and the people he was calling were the people the system rejected: sinners, the blind, pagans, vagrants, the outcasts, the ones "good" people wouldn't contaminate themselves with. The miracles Jesus worked among them were signs that something new was afoot, something they had to be able to read—and something that began with the poor. This was the great sign. Just as two thousand years ago it was in Bethlehem, the "least of all the cities of Judah," that the new age dawned, so now it was in La Fosa, Tutunichapa, San Antonio, San Ramón, Zona Norte, Zona Sur, the smallest, most forgotten places, that new signs abounded to challenge our eyes to read what God was doing in God's people.

Pebble in Your Shoe?

> *When the poor believe in the poor,*
> *That's when we'll be free to sing;*
> *When the poor believe in the poor,*
> *Sisters' and brothers' songs will ring.*
>
> *When the poor seek out the poor,*
> *And we're all for organization,*
> *Then will come our liberation.*
> *When the poor proclaim to the poor*
> *The hope that Jesus gave us,*
> *That's the Kingdom that will save us.*
> —Recessional of the Salvadoran Mass of the People

Only together, united, could we work genuine signs of God's kingdom. But the road was long and hard. We felt that we were too weak. We saw that we were very poor, and we didn't believe in ourselves.

Our community journey made us feel, painfully, that we were

sinners, capable of doing each other harm. The community "acolytes" had an important job to do. They had to smooth the way to
our self-knowledge, so that we could all trace the roots of our evil,
our sin. To accomplish this, they used the parable of the pebble.

Once upon a time there was a general. He knew that a war was
about to break out, and he wanted to get acquainted with his
troops, wanted to find out what condition his soldiers were in. He
set up a rigorous training program, which included long marches.

He sent for one of his battalions and explained the gravity of the
situation and the need to keep in shape. Everybody agreed, and it
was decided that the battalion should go on a three days' march.

The next morning the troops mustered for the march. They were
in great spirits and were singing their battle songs. Their packs were
light on their backs and they swung along with vigor and gusto.

Then all at once a little pebble leapt into the boot of one of the
soldiers. At first it was just a little bother. Soon the pebble began to
dig into the soldier's foot. The march became difficult for this
soldier, but he was unwilling to stop to remove the pebble. What
would the others say—that he had "lady feet"? He didn't want to
be made fun of. He tried not to limp, but the pebble pressed deeper
and deeper into his flesh. The smile left his face. There was no more
singing for this soldier now. He barely bore up under the pain,
nothing more. His only desire was that no one would notice what
was happening.

Suddenly it began to seem to this soldier that the march was
stupid, the general was crazy, they were going to lose the war
anyway, and so on. He started to criticize. By the end of the day
there was nothing that escaped his criticism.

When a halt was called for the night, the soldier could see that a
Red Cross station had been set up, just in case anyone had any
marching problems. He decided not to have his foot looked at.
Everybody would think that all his criticism was just because of the
pebble in his boot! No, he would play the "tough guy"—he didn't
need anybody's help.

During the night, while his comrades slept, the soldier got up—
and went looking for pebbles to put in his comrades' boots so that
they would all feel as he did and there would be an end to this
wretched march.

Our parable came out of the painful experience of what was

wrong in our community. The road we had to march was a long one, and the tiniest pebble that got in our boot and was not quickly removed could do us a great deal of harm. We could end up causing harm to others.

So we needed a "Red Cross station," the sacrament of penance, to prepare us again and again for the journey and for the war, which we knew was coming. We began to rehabilitate this great sacrament of reconciliation. The applause that greeted each penitent on confessing his or her pebble was a real sign of brotherly and sisterly communion.

The community "acoloytes" had a big job ahead of them. They were to prepare the way for all the members of the community to get to know themselves, to confess their faults, and then to keep marching with the seal of God's forgiveness on their forehead.

Temptations in the Wilderness

Believing means not staying in Egypt. It means going out into the wilderness. It means leaving your country, your tribe, your mother and father, and heading out for the Beyond. Belief is the opposite of "Stay where you are, don't budge." By faith, Paul says, Abraham abandoned everything, and left for another land without even knowing where he was headed. In the strength of his faith, Moses went to Pharaoh and said, "It is time for us to go." Believing, in the Bible, is always leaving. Believing is living in tents in the open, with no place you can call your own, and with nothing but a rock to lay your head on. Life's yardstick is not in the past, but in what is to come. This is Israel's faith. And the gospel follows this same line.

Further: believing is always victory over the fundamental tendencies of human beings to be totally preoccupied with their own self-defense. To believe is to be torn up by the roots. Believing means not holding on, but letting go. Not keeping, but giving up. Whoever puts hand to the plow and looks back is of no use to the kingdom of God, Jesus tells us. New wine must be put in new vessels. Those who lose their lives find them. There is risk before there is gain. And take nothing with you on the way—no money, no sack, no shoes. The

religion of maintenance, of protection, and of return to the
maternal womb, is pre-evangelical. The gospel asks us to free
ourselves from what we have, from what we are. The seed
must be sown, the child must grow up and leave home, the
sheep must go out in the midst of wolves. It is not the prodigal
son who is reproached. It is the one who stayed home.
   —Jan Nieuwenhuis, *Si tu hijo te pregunta . . .*

God was not only present among us, but also went on ahead of
us. Along any road to liberation, God takes the lead. But we are
afraid. It's hard to make a break with our securities. We'd like to go
back to Egypt. We'd like a shorter, easier road.

Here the temptation of the lottery loomed. All a person needed
was one ticket. The prize would be entry into the promised land.
Everything would be solved. The poor live by this dream, fall into
this temptation. They take the only money they have, the only
money with which they can take responsibility for themselves or for
one another, and they wager it on that dream. They lose their
chance to grow, and they lose their money.

I'll never forget the meeting we spent reflecting on the lottery
temptation. I said I begged God every day to keep any member
of our community from winning the lottery. They didn't understand. I said I was sure that a prize like that would break up our
solidarity. They said it wouldn't. "Cash like that'll take care of
everybody's troubles here, you'll see." And they all began telling all
the things they would do if they won the lottery. First of all, they'd
all pay a few debts; then they'd give the rest to the community!

Two weeks later, Victor won a big prize. First he started missing
meetings. Then he left the housing co-op. "Why, Victor? What's
going on with you?" Victor said he wanted to make room for poor
people, so he'd bought his own piece of property. Temptation had
defeated him. The community had plenty to think about, with the
case of the lottery and Victor.

There was also the temptation of alcohol because life was still
hard. "When things are this bad, can't you forget about it for a
minute with a little swig? Why not be like everybody else? And not
hold back all the time . . ." The temptation was to do as everybody
does: have a little drink in the bar and a little fun with the ladies
once in a while. How hard it was to swim against the tide!

Traditional religion, too, turned into a strong temptation. "You mean a Corpus Christi procession and a pilgrimage to the shrine of the patron saint every year and lighting candles and all that isn't enough? You mean God isn't satisified with that?" The temptation was to tarry along the way, to adore the golden calf, to abandon the road and be unfaithful to such a demanding God—who called you to a commitment and a journey and refused to let you sink roots anywhere.

In the midst of all these trials, sweltering under the sun of this temptation-crammed wilderness, we had to find a way to protect ourselves. The service the community "deacons" rendered was to defend the community against these temptations.

A first deaconship was that of the readers and acolytes themselves, who cleared up minds and wills so that they could grasp and accept the signs of God's kingdom. A second deaconship was something like marching orders, our rule of life. We were constantly reformulating and revising our rule of life according to circumstances, according to our experiences, and in accordance with what God gave our community to feel at the moment. We had to review our community life and the life of each individual one of us constantly. We asked all of our members to keep their minds open to reality, their hearts ready for prayer so as to be able to hear God, their hands ready to work at whatever concrete things life demanded, and their whole selves open to constant contact with others, especially with the poor.

A third form of deaconship was to further the signs of the kingdom that had appeared among us, with technical and technological means. A wealth of courses began to spring up in the community. The Catholic University began to offer courses in theology for our people, and we started nursing courses that produced deacons in the form of travelling practical nurses. We began literacy courses for adults, using Paulo Freire's method, and even had experts come in and adapt the primers for our use. There were courses in cooperatives, and others on sewing and clothes-making. These were all ways of protecting and preserving the miracles being worked in our midst.

Despite all these efforts, however, people fell by the wayside. In spite of all the help available to them from the acolytes and deacons, they couldn't stand the desert sun and fell ill. We had a deaconship to perform among them too. The community visited the "sick," these persons who had become alienated from the group, to tell them that we needed them, to remind them that there was a place for them among us. With the oil of friendship and love we healed their wounds.

As we worked out our deaconship, we found that the church needed some new doors. Up until now, we had had only one: courses of initiation. But there were the "sick" now, comrades who for various reasons had withdrawn from the campaign. Our pastoral ministry to the "sick" made us realize that we had to open different doors for them. They couldn't start over from the beginning. Neither could they share all the commitments we had by now, since they had already fallen under them. We needed new ways.

One of the doors we opened then was theater. We put on a play called *Awakening of a People* written by communities in Panama. We put it on, then we asked those who had fallen away what they thought about it.

As we tried to rescue the alienated, we also discovered a sense of the sacrament of the sick. It usually is only associated with death and serious illness, but it actually had to do with the daily life of the community, so full of temptations, falls, and efforts to start all over again.

Happy the Persecuted for Justice

It is an obvious fact, then, that our church has been persecuted over the last three years. But what is more important is why it has been persecuted. It is not just the random priest or institution that has been persecuted or attacked. The persecution and attacks have been directed against that part of the church that has taken sides with the poor and come out in their defense. Again we find the key to an understanding of the persecution of the church: the poor. Again it is the poor who show us what is really happening.

The church has gained an understanding of this persecution by living it from the point of view of the poor. This persecution has been occasioned by a defense of the poor; we are simply suffering the fate of the poor themselves.

—Archbishop Romero, Louvain, Feb. 2, 1980

Rodolfo had never missed a meeting. Then one day he stopped coming. I went over to see him, and was told that he was in jail. Rodolfo worked in a factory. The manager wanted him to quit and be rehired. This would mean losing eleven years' seniority. It would mean starting all over again. Rodolfo refused to quit. He invoked the labor laws: if he were released from his contract, they would have to pay him eleven months' wages. So they accused him of stealing 120 colons and had him thrown in jail. If he valued his liberty he would sign a waiver of employment and compensation. He explained all this to me when I went down to jail to visit him. I went to speak to the manager, a very "Catholic" type. I stood up for Rodolfo, said I would take responsibility for the theft and make restitution, and begged him to give my friend another chance. But the manager was unmoved. Both the manager and his attorney (also very "Catholic") would have nothing but Rodolfo's waiver. I told them they were Pharisees, and they told me I was a subversive.

The powerful were keeping an eye on us more and more. A kindergarten was being built for the children. The order came from the social worker at the ministry: "This work will not proceed unless there is help from the people of the communities." It was likewise impossible to get the ministry to give official recognition to our housing co-op, one of the most relevant signs of the growth of our communities. We weren't trusted. The government spied on us to see what "sort" we were, how we thought, where we got our funds.

Manolo was called in by the director of his company and questioned about us and about his participation in the community. He was told then and there that he'd be fired if he kept up his "subversive" activities. With Arsenio it was worse. They hauled him in and interrogated him about the communities. After three days they let him go. (He was all the stronger for his trial.) A police officer came to Ricardo's house, drunk, to find out about the community directors and the meetings.

The community battle to defend those who were behind in their mortgage payments was one of our many conflicts. We were accused of fomenting disorder. It was the same with the literacy campaign. We used the Freire method. But Freire was a "notorious

Communist," they said, and so they began to keep us under surveillance. Our work was becoming more risky by the day—which made it more Christian.

Chico the Burning Bush

Moses was looking after the flock of Jethro, his father-in-law, priest of Midian. He led his flock to the far side of the wilderness and came to Horeb, the mountain of God. There the angel of Yahweh appeared to him in the shape of a flame of fire, coming from the middle of a bush. Moses looked; there was the bush blazing but it was not being burned up. "I must go and look at this strange sight," Moses said, "and see why the bush is not burned." Now Yahweh saw him go forward to look, and God called to him from the middle of the bush. "Moses, Moses!" he said. "Here I am," he answered. "Come no nearer," he said. "Take off your shoes, for the place on which you stand is holy ground. I am the God of your father," he said, "the God of Abraham, the God of Isaac and the God of Jacob." At this Moses covered his face, afraid to look at God.

And Yahweh said, "I have seen the miserable state of my people in Egypt. I have heard their appeal to be free of their slave drivers. Yes, I am well aware of their sufferings. I mean to deliver them out of the hands of the Egyptians and bring them up out of that land to a land rich and broad, a land where milk and honey flow, the home of the Canaanites, the Hittites, the Amorites, the Perizzites, the Hivites and the Jebusites. And now the cry of the sons of Israel has come to me, and I have witnessed the way in which the Egyptians oppress them, so come, I send you to Pharaoh to bring the sons of Israel, my people, out of Egypt."

—Exodus 3:1–10

God was being manifested to us by miraculous signs. We discovered that our communities were a people called to proclaim God in history by serving that history and by anticipating the kingdom of God in signs. It was in the midst of the first persecutions that we discovered our vocation to liberate the people.

To have a housing co-op we first had to clear the land, level it, and stake it out in lots. So we needed surveyors. A surveyor belonged to one of our communities, and he set to work. But there was too much to do. He started working overtime, but he told us he'd never finish even so. Then he asked for help from the university. The dean of the College of Agriculture put us in contact with a teacher, the teacher introduced us to Chico.

From that start, Chico showed himself to be the finest symbol of dedication and toil that we had ever known. He never took a day off, not even on weekends. He spent months measuring off and dividing up the lots. At night he would sketch out on paper what he'd done in the fields during the day. He would work right with our people, swinging a pickax or wielding a shovel. He was simply indefatigable. It was all volunteer work, and his generous, tireless unselfishness was astounding. He would let other jobs go to help us instead. Chico became a challenge to the whole community. He was a "burning bush that was not burned up," a giver of self that didn't burn out. And from the midst of this bush, we heard the word of the Lord.

Like Moses, we had been saved from the waters of death by that first encounter of Christian initiation. But our life had really been rather tranquil ever since. Oh, now and then we'd wax indignant at the injustices suffered by our people or at some particular conflict or other. But generally we were pretty much wrapped up in ourselves and our own problems. Now here was this stranger, not even a member of our community, working for us tirelessly day and night. We understood what the sign of Chico meant and we were afraid—just as Moses was afraid when he discovered what his own rescue was going to mean in terms of a call. We understood that if we just stuck with our housing co-op, we'd be stuck with ourselves. We'd stay locked up in ourselves. Chico's dedication showed us a larger vocation. The liberation of a people. A whole people.

We used our meetings to reflect on the sign that was Chico, on Chico's challenge for the future. We had come to a crossroads. There were four ways we could go. We could simply be glad of Chico's help and glad that he was winning heaven with it. We could praise and admire Chico as an exceptional case, a unique person. We could take up his challenge and start working harder and better, for instance by starting new co-ops. Or . . . we could use his sign as an occasion to call our whole lives into question and rediscover our calling as mission. We could leave our sheep, head straight for Pharaoh, and make him let the Salvadoran people go, make him release them from their misery and injustice.

We took the fourth way. We accepted the challenge of this bright-burning bush and began to be more missionary. We did not know then how soon we would be meeting up with the forces of death.

CHAPTER THREE

Hour of Trial

The Chains of Sin

Now we have a better notion of sin. We know that offense to God is the death of the human being. We know that sin is truly "mortal—not only because of the interior death of the one committing it, but because of the real, objective death it produces. And this reminds us of a profound datum of our Christian faith: Sin is what put God's Son to death, and sin continues to be what puts God's sons and daughters to death.

This basic truth of Christian faith is something we see daily in situations in our country. God cannot be offended without offense to one's sister or brother. And the worst offense to God, the worst of secularisms, is, as one of our theologians has said, "converting God's sons and daughters, temples of the Holy Spirit, the historical Body of Christ, into victims of oppression and injustice, into slaves of economic appetites, into the torn and tattered starvelings of political oppression."
—Archbishop Romero, Louvain, Feb. 2, 1980

On August 22, 1974, at 11:30 P.M., seven men in civilian garb came into our house carrying machine guns. They bound our hands and feet, made us lie face down on the floor, and held the barrels of their guns at the backs of our heads. They examined everything in the house, and took anything they wanted. The assault lasted half an hour. They cut the phone wires and spoke among themselves like thieves. A few days later we found out they were from a paramilitary group. In two weeks, Benitón, a boy in the community who had "disappeared," was released. He told us how he had been tortured and interrogated about the community. Under torture, he had consented to make a drawing of our house and sign a blank sheet of paper they could use against us.

Things were hard in El Salvador now. Priests were being blacklisted and threatened or taken hostage. Schoolteachers were persecuted. Co-ops were being closely watched. Peasant leaders and union organizers were thrown in prison. University professors and political opposition leaders had to leave the country and the university was closed. Slanderous attacks against our base communities grew apace, and Archbishop Chávez and Bishop Rivera were called the "red bishops." It was the hour of trial. Now we, too, began to understand what sin is. Nothing was happening "by accident."

At first, of course, we could scarcely imagine why there should be such persecutions. Why should there be such strong opposition to the poor improving their lives? If what we had been doing was right, then why were we officially persecuted by authorities styling themselves "Christian"? We still lacked the insight to give a correct answer to these questions. The community "doorkeepers" had a lot of teaching and explaining to do before we came to understand.

The case of Felix helped a great deal. Felix was in his teens, the second of nine children. Nobody in his family had a job, and we couldn't understand how they managed to survive. Then Rodolfo got Felix a job as a bricklayer's helper. Felix showed up for work, then came to us for advice.

"What shall I do? The boss says I start next week. He took me on because Rodolfo asked him. But to make room for me he has to fire another guy. I don't know what to do. I need the job to help my family. But so does the other guy! What should I do?"

No one in the community could answer him. The only answer was a cruel one: One person's bread is another person's death. I remember that this was when we started reflecting more deeply on personal sin and what the structures of sin are. The "sin of this world" in John's Gospel is structural sin, and it is terribly strongly rooted in capitalist society.

In a situation of widespread unemployment, as in El Salvador today, anyone who manages to find work deprives another person of that work. Without committing any personal fault, we are all swept along by this sin—and it is a mortal sin, since it causes many deaths.

If you go to school, somebody else can't. If you own your own home, somebody else doesn't. If you go to the doctor, somebody else won't be seen. If you eat, you are taking bread out of some-body else's mouth. In El Salvador, schools are the privilege of one small group. There aren't enough doctors. Most of the people live in slums. This is a situation of mortal sin.

We felt so helpless in the face of all this! We were all bound down by sin, we were all chained to a sinful system dedicated to the service of the great god Money. Our architects designed houses only for those who can afford them. Our doctors only treat people who can pay. Schools only open their doors to those who can pay the tuition. Our best land is used to raise crops for export—crops that bring in foreign capital, while our people go hungry and we have to import beans and rice.

And so we understood, for the first time, that when Jesus drove the buyers and sellers out of the Temple he was not doing it to hurt the small business people who were selling their little items or changing 25-colon bills. He was angry with a whole corrupt system of hoarding and profiting in the name of God.

It was a system like that, an oppressive, blasphemous system, that was persecuting us, and testing the faith, hope, and love that we had stored up since forming our communities.

Conflict Builds New Dedication . . .

In a society whose ideals are power, possession, and pleasure, I pray that I may be a sign of what it really means to love. I will do my best to be a sign that Christ Jesus alone is Lord of history—that he is present here in our midst—and that he is capable of inspiring a love mightier than our own instincts, mightier than all of the economic and political forces, mightier than death itself. My one desire is to lead a life in the following of Christ —he who was poor, chaste, and obedient to the will of his Father. I wish to live for him alone and his saving work, as his disciple.

I promise our Lord that I will be faithful—in sickness and in health, in youth and old age, in tranquillity and persecution, in joy and in sorrow. I promise to do my best to share in his incarnation among the poorest of the poor, and to imitate his poverty and solidarity with them in their liberation struggle. This is my hope and desire: to share in his evangelizing mission among human beings, concentrating all the power of my will and affections on him and on all my sisters and brothers, and living in continual quest of the Father's will: in his word, in the church, in the signs of the times, and in the poor.

—The Vows pronounced by Silvia Arriola
in the presence of the base Christian communities and
of Archbishop Oscar Arnulfo Romero of San Salvador.
Silvia was murdered Jan. 18, 1981.

Conflict and trial touched us all, but in widely varying ways. Many religious women found their work the occasion of serious conflict in their communities.

Ever since coming to El Salvador, I had served as chaplain for the sisters who conducted a school for girls. A number of these young women, aspirants to the religious life, lived with the sisters in their community. The aspirants studied the Bible with me, and served as religion teachers for the children of our parish.

All of this led to some self-examination on the part of the aspirants. Some of them went to the community with a new concern: "We are from very poor families," they said. "But it looks as if what we are going to be doing is teaching rich kids."

And thereby hangs a tale. In November 1970, three of the aspirants left the convent and went looking for a room. They found one. Then one of the young women got a job as a seamstress. All three lived on her earnings and went to school, studying together in the evenings. At first they slept on the floor, sometimes with nothing to eat and nothing to drink but plain water.

Soon they decided to become full-fledged members of our community, and I suddenly found myself the chaplain of a new convent. In a few months a fourth woman joined them. And so we kept up our Bible study, the celebration of the Eucharist, and our pastoral work.

On three different occasisons, our new convent was on the brink of dissolving. The first time it was because the little house in which the young women rented their room was going to be torn down to make way for a commercial structure. The second time it was because of threats from some drunken men. And the third time it was because they couldn't pay the rent.

But the young women got their college degrees and began to devote themselves to full-time pastoral work. Two of them pronounced their vows before the parish council. Gradually these young women became the mothers of that hopeless slum. A miracle was occurring. Women were keeping men in line! Women were directing a community. What ought to have been impossible in our macho society became possible through the generous love of a new and different sort of nun.

The number of sisters grew to seven. Their lifestyle was one of solidarity with all. The distinction between man and woman, Christian and non-Christian, pure and impure, went by the board. Their poverty was not heroic self-denial, a test of their love of God. It was a necessity, for they were fighting for the liberation of the poor. Their chastity was not a No to desire. It was a way of living perpetual availability to others. Their obedience was not the abdication of their own will in favor of that of their superiors. It was coresponsibility to the will of God, a God who spoke to them in history and the signs of the times. Their prayer was not the supplication of persons seeking magical solutions to gigantic problems. It was their self-offering to God, in search, in trust (but in protest too)—and in hope against hope.

To the poor, this novelty, these women strong in their weakness, came as no surprise at all.

. . . And a New Liturgy

One day when John's disciples and the Pharisees were fasting, some people came and said to him, "Why is it that John's disciples and the disciples of the Pharisees fast, but your disciples do not?" Jesus replied, "Surely the bridegroom's attendants would never think of fasting while the bridegroom is still with them? As long as they have the bridegroom with them, they could not think of fasting. But the time will come for the bridegroom to be taken away from them, and then, on that day, they will fast. No one sews a piece of unshrunken cloth on an old cloak; if he does, the patch pulls away from it, the new from the old, and the tear gets worse. And nobody puts new wine into old wineskins; if he does, the wine will burst the skins, and the wine is lost and the skins too. No! New wine, fresh skins!"

—Mark 2:18–22

What conflict there was! What a scandal it was to see these new expressions of our faith! We began to exercise a bit of creativity in the Eucharistic liturgy. We held dialogues on the readings, and we began to express our joy, our gratitude, our sorrow, in new songs. Protest songs began to ring out in church—songs protesting the "sin of the world," which we were coming to know in dramatic intensity. The greeting of peace became a high point in the celebration. The holy kiss was "hail and farewell" from each to all.

All of this was a great scandal. "How can you pray with a racket like that? What kind of recollection can there be with all that jumping around? Why put political songs in something as sacred as the Mass? What's all the clapping about? What saint are you clapping for? Why do you have to be chattering about repression, exploitation, and injustice when you're supposed to be praising God? Why this boundless irreverence?" These were age-old questions of the Pharisees and scribes—alive and well after all these centuries—who cannot bear the aroma of new wine, and who refuse to give up old garments and old bodies.

This was the birth of the *Misa Popular Salvadoreña,* the Mass of the Salvadoran People. Our Mass was born of the daily experience of our communities. Behind each song was a flesh-and-blood story. The Lord Have Mercy was a brazen scream to God after the murder of Father Octavio Ortiz, his head crushed by an army tank.

Lord, have mercy.
Lord, have mercy on your people.
The Lord hears the cries of Abel's spilt blood,
The sobs of the people awakened in Moses
The same shout born in our entrails,
That a thousand strokes of cunning would stifle.

Lord, injustice afflicts and oppresses us:
Hasten to our side!
We are the lowly,
And boots and tanks
Smash in their fury
The faces of those who live and die
For us and for you.

The Lamb of God was simply a translation of our actual experience. Those who commit themselves to the poor in a world as unjust as the one in which we live will both suffer and conquer.

Jesus spoke of his peace. So did we:

You were slaughtered on the cross,
and conquered the evil of the world,
    you denounced the unjust oppressor
    and raised the poor from the dust:
We beseech you, hear us,
for you hear the cry of your people.

You were slaughtered on the cross,
murdered by the powerful;
today once more you spill your blood
    in the blood of our fallen.
You were slaughtered on the cross,
builder of peace with justice.
Help us not to weaken in the struggle
    for the coming of your kingdom.

May your peace be ours,
    from the day we cause justice to bloom
    like Aaron's staff.

The new Mass with its new hymns provoked conflict, but it could not be stopped. Bishop Romero asked a popular poet to write a hymn to Jesus the Divine Savior, the patron of El Salvador. This hymn became the Glory to God of the *Misa Popular:*

Vibrant our songs, explosions of joy!
I must join my people, there in the cathedral.
Thousands of voices are one this day,
Feast of *El Salvador,* our Savior.

Glory, Lord,
Glory, Lord,
Glory to the patron of El Salvador!
In no other lord is redemption—
One patron, ours: Our Savior Divine!

Because you are just
And defend the poor,
Because you love us
And are truly our friend—
We come today, all your people here,
Firm and determined,
To proclaim our worth and dignity.

Lord, once more you will be glorified
As of old on Mount Tabor
when you shall see
This people transformed
With life and liberty in El Salvador!

But the gods of power and money
to this transfiguration say, "No!"
And this, Lord, we know, is why
Your strong right arm
Is the first to be raised
Against their oppression.

These were the new "wineskins," the new vessels that we were fashioning to hold our new faith. Of course, it was the old faith of the prophets, who were so committed to the program of a God whose works are works of justice. It was the eternal faith in Jesus, the fulfiller of that faith, the pioneer in the supreme act of his faith: the giving of one's own life for others.

Conflict with Bishop Romero

> *If the church makes of itself an institution, it succeeds as the Pharisees succeeded: It turns God's words into its own property, into a code of laws, customs, and formulas with which to identify.*
>
> —José Comblin, *Sent from the Father*

Before he became El Salvador's great prophet and martyr, Archbishop Romero was in conflict with our communities. Before his conversion, we were a stumbling block to him.

For instance, when President Molina ordered the closing of the national university in 1972, an article appeared in the papers signed by the then Secretary of the Salvadoran Bishops' Conference, Bishop Romero, to the effect that it was a good idea to close down such a hotbed of communist activities. Our communities were indignant. Not only had the university been closed, but the people who lived in the slum across the street from the university had been evicted from their homes. The shacks were simply destroyed and some of the people who had lived in them were put in jail. A great number of university employees, members of our communities, were beaten, and members of the academic administration were thrown out of their offices in an incredible display of violence. How could the bishops praise that? We were sure that neither Bishop Chávez nor Bishop Rivera would applaud such barbarity.

A great conflict arose in the communities, which became a boiling pot of reflection and discussions. Were we going to keep silent and simply stand in awe of the bishops' words? Or were we going to raise our voices and condemn this interference with the university?

We wrote a letter to Bishop Romero. We listed our observations and criticisms, and invited him to come and share our Eucharist, and we would all reflect on the situation together. The bishop did come to our parish, but so much conflict arose that the Mass had to be stopped. What happened was that after the readings and homily we began to question the bishops' stance. "Do the bishops know everything that happened? Whom did they consult before they spoke? What becomes of the gospel in this document?"

The people referred to the Medellín document. On the basis of that document, they rejected the episcopal communiqué. Bishop Romero defended himself by quoting a letter from a Chilean bishop that we had never heard of. Then he accused us of disobedience to ecclesiastical authorities and of mixing politics with the Eucharist. We continued our own line of argument. We cited Medellín, and we asked Bishop Romero why the church was always on the side of the rich. Why didn't the church associate with the victims of repression? This would help it make more realistic judgments. The atmosphere became extremely tense. Then the bishop said that this was not a Eucharist but a political meeting.

I became so indignant that I said, "My friends, His Excellency is right. We can't celebrate the Eucharist in an atmosphere like this. How can we give thanks to our Lord for the call of our faith when we're forbidden any dialogue with our superiors? Let's end the celebration here. Perhaps at some later time it may be possible to have this dialogue and this celebration." I took off my alb and stole, but the discussion went on, hot and explosive.

The next day we went to see Bishop Rivera. We told him what had happened and asked his help. He promised to come to see us, and he did.

When Bishop Romero became Archbishop of San Salvador, he was converted, and he came back to our communities. The "prodigal son" was the father this time! And his return was a festival of reconciliation.

Change Hearts or Society?

This nearness to the world of the poor, as we see, will be both an incarnation and a conversion. Changes have been needed in the church—in our pastoral activity, in our education, in our religious and priestly life, and in our lay movements. We have not managed to make these changes, because our eyes have been riveted on the church alone. We have been turned inward. Now we shall be able to make these changes, because we have turned outward—turned to the world of the poor.
                          —Archbishop Romero, Louvain, Feb. 2, 1980

We discovered the "sin of the world," and we were startled and terrified. The demons were different now. Many of them were clothed in the feelings of powerlessness that came over you when you feel yourself to be confronted with an overwhelming task. Up until now, our community exorcism had consisted mostly of expelling demons from the hearts of individuals. Now it was other demons, those demons that live in the network of the social structure, that challenged us.

About this time, the popular organizations became organized for systematic struggle and consciousness-raising. This was a new weapon which would enable the poor to confront the power of the mighty. *Campesinos,* union members, students, teachers, "marketplace women," catechists, community directors—all of us felt the upheaval and challenge of this new movement in El Salvador. The popular organizations looked like the right tool to drive out the demons living in the very roots of society—demons more powerful than the ones that burrow into the individual human heart.

This network of new organizations raised new questions for us. Were they any business of ours? Would these organizations unite or divide us? Some of the members of our communities were joining them. Others stayed at the level of collaborators, or sympathizers. Still others were paralyzed by fear.

In our meetings, the "readers" continued to interpret God's reality. They were our consultants, our "orientators." What did our consciences, the community, the Bible, and the poor say about this new phenomenon of the popular organizations?

Some of us were of the opinion that the first thing to do was to fashion a new heart for the new human being—and only then attempt to renew society. Others "read," in our harsh Salvadoran reality, that if our society did not have new roots, the new human being would never be born. All of us saw clearly that the option for the poor was the main thing in Jesus' gospel. But where to begin?

Gradually we discovered that the dichotomy between personal conversion and social transformation was a false one. After all, behind every personal conversion is, at least in seed, a social commitment. At the same time, of course, no social commitment is possible without a corresponding conversion of heart. The correct solution to this false dilemma, then, was a personal, interior commitment to the social task.

So it came about that many, very many, of the people in our

communities, moved by God's Spirit, threw themselves into the struggle with the demons of this sinful social system and became full-fledged members of the burgeoning popular organizations.

We had discovered that the God of history is crucified in every person that the system exploits. And so our personal commitment to change was gradually becoming an option for a social and political program consistent with the intent of Jesus' gospel.

Now new subjects came up in our discussions, boiling and bubbling. What should we do about the elections? What can we do about the new high prices for basic commodities? What attitude should we adopt toward the new guerilla movements?

I'll never forget the Miss Universe contest in San Salvador, when the police went around picking up starving kids and beggars so they wouldn't spoil the grand fiesta. At one point the contestants changed out of their bikinis and were bused to San Miguel Cathedral. Day and night, the only thing they ever heard about was this "land of smiles" of ours. What a perfect picture of the "sin of this world."

We lived in a world wrapped in false beauty and joy.

In a flash, we saw that the "acolytes" of our communities were going to have to go out to the highways and byways of our land and be Good Samaritans to the stricken—those the system had struck down and left for dead. The reason so many were in need was that a handful of the comfortable had marginalized them. The reason there were poor, so many poor, in El Salvador was that there were rich, a few rich, who monopolized everything.

It looks simple as we look back on it. But at the time it was a crucial discovery. El Salvador is the "country of the fourteen families"—the land of the Llaches, the De Solas, the Hills, the Dueñas, the Regalados, the Wrights, the Salaverrías, the García Prietos, the Quiñonezes, the Guirolas, the Borjas, the Sols, the Daglios, and the Meza Ayaus. And the differences between these few families and the countless others was a shameful scandal. For the directors of our communities,—our "readers" of the word of God in life, in history—in *this* history and in *this* country—the exact direction to take was not easy to discern. Jesus' message had been spiritualized and individualized to the point that its subversive force had been neutralized. Nor was it so simple to unmask the system that had kidnapped not only the gospel but all of life's precious words, had raped them, stripped them of their meaning and given them some other meaning. There was election fraud and we heard "democracy." We heard about our "native land" and it was the private property of the fourteen families and their armed militias. We heard of "God," and in the same breath were told God blessed an army of murderers and threw the poor in jail. In the name of "peace," tanks were purchased. And every year Independence Day was celebrated in a country of slaves.

Our faith was still weak and immature and we took scandal when we saw pictures of the pope's ambassador, the nuncio, drinking champagne with the generals, or of one of our bishops wearing a colonel's uniform for the Feast of Jesus our Savior, and sitting in the front row with the rest of the worldly dignitaries. Was this the same Jesus that we believed in?

Our exorcists and readers had quite a job to do! Theirs would be the task of leading us in this unfair, unequal battle. Theirs would be the task of nourishing our hope, and inspiring us with the courage of David in the hour of Goliath.

The Bible and the Newspapers

This hope fostered by the church is not naive, nor is it passive. It is a call, issued through the word of God, to the poor majority, to accept their responsibility. It is a call for their conscientization, a call for their organization, even though they live in a country where all this is illegal, or at least highly imprudent and dangerous. The hope fostered by the church is a mainstay and support, sometimes a crucial one, for the poor in their just causes and just demands. The hope we preach to the poor is hope for the restoration of their dignity. The hope we preach to the poor is the courage to become the authors of their own destiny.

In sum, then: the church has not only turned to the poor, it has made them the special addressees of its whole mission. For, as Puebla says: "God takes up their defense. He loves them."

—Archbishop Romero, Louvain, Feb. 2, 1980

In a world as dark and threatening as ours, it was urgent that we prepare our people for service, real service in a just, complex cause. The Department of Theology of the Catholic University, the Central American University, set up theology courses to help our people perform this service in mature faith and realistic hope. Nearly 150 members of our communities enrolled in these courses. Two evenings a week we studied the message of Jesus and the mission of the church. It was a sacrifice to go to night school but it soon became a great joy. We began to see our commitment more clearly. We who were taking the courses committed ourselves to multiplying what we were learning by sharing it with those who couldn't go. We changed our weekly meeting schedule to accommodate the classes. Our "acolytes" became the theologians of the people, with their Bible under one arm and their newspaper under the other. They were performing their task of "discerning reality" with the new eyes that the Spirit of Jesus gives the poor. The persecution was becoming more severe. The militias and paramilitary groups were becoming more and more repressive. In our pain, we finally saw which way we should go.

We were all enrolled in a kind of accelerated apprenticeship. There was a lot of tension. We noted with a good deal of concern that practically only the youth, the unmarried could carry on this struggle with the world's sin and not falter. Responsibility for their children was hamstringing the efforts of married couples— however much they might have committed themselves to our mission. If you were seen at a protest rally you were out of a job, and if you were out of a job you were watching your children starve to death. If you tried to join the union you could very easily end up in jail and be tortured and killed, and what would become of your children then?

A sacrament is a sign of God's presence. So one sacrament shouldn't conflict with another. But here the sacrament of marriage was in conflict with the sacrament of service to the poor. Something was wrong. What? We started looking for the answer, looking for a solution. Our communities set out to meet the challenge to create conditions in which married love would not conflict with social commitment.

The solution we discovered was what we called a "solidarity

fund." We started a kind of family co-op. We bought things in common, took care of the chidren in common, and had some savings in common. The parish team put its money into the common fund, and everybody's income and expenses were administered in community fashion. Couples on fixed wages, with solid jobs and two incomes, still felt privileged, but now nobody could say anything, since both incomes went into the solidarity fund. We were all equals now, since we all lived on equal resources.

So we each opened our purses and discovered that together we could make it possible for our married couples to love each other and risk their lives for others all at the same time. We saw that to make this possible was a responsibility to be shared by everybody. This was a revelation to us, and gave us a lot of courage. It warmed our hearts, and made them strong.

Murder: Not Just in the Movies Now

Many of his followers said, "This is intolerable language. How could anyone accept it?" . . . After this, many of his disciples left him and stopped going with him.
—John 6:60–66

This was a time of community redefinition. Everything was getting worse for our communities. Arrests, kidnappings, torture, prison—all this was on the rise. It was all we talked about. We were living in dangerous times.

The hour of our marvelous, consoling signs was past. It was the hour of the sword, and we had to believe that the forces of life would prevail against those of death.

About this same time, a wave of North American religious sects were invading the country. These new religious groups preached a spiritual "salvation" one of "peace and happiness." They closed their eyes to the scenario of sin and death being played out before them. And some of us succumbed to that easy temptation—the temptation to believe that you are serving God just by praying and reading the Bible and not getting involved in any one's problems. The sects insisted that this was the "true religion," the religion that led to God. Many of our members tried to convince themselves of this, abandoning the road the communities had chosen. These charismatic sects accused us of being mere politicians, manipulators of the faith. They insisted that the church had to be "neutral." The temptation was very strong.

I can still hear Rogelio: "For years we've been talking in these meetings about Jesus' death and resurrection. Every Sunday we celebrate these events. But we've never let death into our lives. We see death from far away, like a movie. Death isn't in our program. And only the poor can teach us this familiarity with death. They're in a life and death struggle, day and night. That's why they're so much like Christ."

Yes, we had to face the possibility of our violent death. Now we began to put a good many intra-church concerns to one side. We became more missionary. Here is what we asked ourselves. Does a Christian follow Jesus in his membership in the Jewish religious institution? Or does a Christian follow Jesus as the one sent by the God? Which is more important, fidelity to the traditional piety of institutionalized religion, or involvement with the world as persons-sent, as daughters and sons of God? Jesus broke with the mentality of traditional piety, and traditional religion. So did the first Christian communities. We too, then, ought to get over our "churchy" mentality and live our faith. New wine needs new containers.

In this daily break with our old mentality, Archbishop Romero was a source of great illumination to us. His homilies, filled with authentic Christian reflection, helped us overcome the temptation to dally along the road, to shut ourselves up inside ourselves. His own sudden conversion helped us make the leap.

Human Rights: A Voice for the Voiceless

> *I've never felt I was a prophet as an individual. No, it's you and I, the people of God, who are a prophetic people. I really have to say, thank God there's a prophetic awakening in our archdiocese: in the basic Christian community, in the group that reflects on God's word. Thank God for this critical consciousness of our Christianity that has appeared in our midst. This will no longer be "crowd Christianity." It will be conscious, conscientious Christianity.*
> —Archbishop Romero, July 1979

El Salvador in these years, like the other countries of Latin America, was under the imperial hegemony of the United States. In our republics, this hegemony took the concrete form of ferocious, repressive "national security" regimes, regimes that marginalized the poor. The "development" model foisted on us by the United States gave a voice only to the privileged few.

Now we were learning, understanding, and assimilating the revelation with which we had been favored: that the most important "deaconship," the most essential service to the church and our communities at that time was the proclamation of human rights. We were eager to become the voice of those who had no voice, and who in that system would never have a voice.

In Archbishop Romero, this service truly took flesh. He was the great deacon, the heroic servant of the people, the incorruptible defender of the rights of the poor. Archbishop Romero's ninety-minute homilies in the cathedral nourished and fortified us as nothing ever had before. He defended the right of the people to organize. He denounced the judiciary and North American imperialism. His were the cries of a prophet—and not only for the Christian community but for the whole people.

Our communities were gathering every Sunday to hear the archbishop's homily which radio station YSAX broadcast all over the country. We gathered strength from his words—strength to speak up, strength to defend our rights and to defend them to the death. The people were getting up on their feet. Their hope was beginning to fly like a banner and burn like the torches we held above our heads high in our night processions.

The people found their voice. They found it in the voice of their bishop. As never before in history, they felt the support of the church. The very stones cried out: all over the walls of the city great books were being written—the slogans of the voice of the people. The will of the people was being expressed in graffiti! The popular organizations took over the churches, using Jesus' own pulpit to let the people's voice be heard. From the step of the Cathedral of Jesus Savior, night and day now, you could hear the cries, the demands of a people who were beginning to speak.

Station YSAX exercised a diaconate, too, with its announcements, its music, and all its programming. The archdiocesan paper,

Orientación, was passed from hand to hand, filling with hope a people who were learning to "get up and walk." The Human Rights Commission took up the Salvadoran people's defense, carrying the voice of the poor to the farthest corners of the earth. The chancery's legal aid service was the tribunal where the poor might make known their pain, and it became the loudspeaker that carried the voice of the poor to countries that had hardly even heard of our little, suffering country.

Then, encouraged by this support on the part of the church, and living with the daily thought of death, we organized a retreat in preparation for the sacrament of confirmation. Now was the moment to step forward as witnesses of Jesus Christ crucified and risen.

These were fantastic days. I remember how we returned from this encounter much less euphoric than we had from our other retreat, the one we had made to prepare for baptism. We were less euphoric but we were more mature. We had made our decision to present ourselves to the bishop to ask for the sacrament of the Spirit, with the Spirit's gifts of understanding, counsel, fortitude, knowledge, piety, and fear of the Lord. For our struggle was going to be a harsh one.

Bishop Chávez laid his hand on many members of our communities. All of them were adults. Chepe, who was in his seventies, was the spokesperson of the group. "Yes, I understand, and I hope to be faithful even to the death if I must."

It was an emotional moment for Bishop Chávez. He had always insisted on confirming small children. Now he started talking about confirmation as the sign of a mature faith. This sacrament challenged us to be faithful to God and to the people in these difficult times. Our ceremony that day brought a great lift to pastoral work in the archdiocese.

Yes, in the hour of trial, we were truly "confirmed"— strengthened for the great act of love: the act of giving one's life for one's friends.

CHAPTER FOUR

Passion, Crucifixion, and Death of the Salvadoran People

Land of Smiles, Kingdom of Death

> *Now my soul is troubled.*
> *What shall I say:*
> *Father, save me from this hour*
> *But it was for the very reason that I have come to this hour.*
>
> *Now the hour has come*
> *for the Son of Man to be glorified.*
> *I tell you, most solemnly,*
> *unless a wheat grain falls on the ground and dies,*
> *it remains only a single grain;*
> *but if it dies,*
> *it yields a rich harvest.*
> *Anyone who loves his life loses it;*
> *anyone who hates his life in this world*
> *will keep it for the eternal life.*
>
> —John 12:27, 24–25

And so we had to accept death. In doing so, we became more and more "people with our people" because El Salvador is a country organized for death.

The women all heard radio propaganda on contraception from morning till night. They were told where and when they could get the products they would need. Doctors were always available to sterilize them. Didn't it hurt to see their children starve to death? They should avoid this, and they would be cooperating in the nation's progress as well. The problem could be solved in a few minutes! International organizations advised this, and gave their assistance.

Sterilizations occur in El Salvador at the rate of twenty to fifty a day. There are fewer mouths crying for beans now, and fewer voices demanding the right to live from the privileged few who already have their human rights. And of course fewer tongues to engage in demands and protest.

There was Sinforosa. Every day she grew thinner and more pale. One day she told me, "Last year the doctor put a thing in me. I said I wasn't going to be sterilized, I still felt young and I didn't want to. So the doctor told me this thing would do the same thing. But I've been bleeding for six months now. They told me it can't be the thing, because that came out. It has to be something else. And they can't find it and I think I'm dying."

We saved her in time—even though the doctors didn't show as much interest in saving her life as when they were trying to stop life. Today Sinforosa has two new children, and she smiles now. The only wealth, the only hope, the only "means of production" that the poor have are their children.

Then there was Minerva. I stopped in to see her one day. She gave me a glass of pineapple juice.

"What's the matter, Minerva?" I asked. "Why are you looking at me so strangely?"

"Can't you see I've got real glasses now instead of plastic ones?"

The new glasses were a symbol of a big, big change in her life.

"I wasn't ever going to get glasses. My old man would have busted them over my head. Now he's in the community, and he's mended his ways. He doesn't drink and shout at me any more the way he used to. So to celebrate I bought these glasses!"

But Minerva wanted to celebrate her liberation with another symbol, too, a more important one. "Look, Padre, now that him and me are gettin' along better, I'd like to have another baby. But they put a thing in me a while back and the doctors tell me it's too late, it's too dangerous to take it out. And they tell me how each kid is more misery."

I managed to get Minerva to a doctor who was genuinely interested, and she had the new child she wanted to have to celebrate her new life.

The children who escape contraception are threatened from birth by the most serious of all diseases: hunger. Most children born in El Salvador die from malnutrition. Even the children who escape death by starvation have to face the constant threat of death. In El Salvador, it's a crime to be young and poor. The regime of death maintained by the successive governments directs its repression especially against the youth. They know that youth has more energy and perceptivity, and that the young are more likely to raise their voices against institutionalized violence or otherwise talk out of turn.

Pancho was a *campesino* refugee. The year was 1979, and the waves of refugees from the countryside to the capital were under way. "Father," he told me, "this is no life. The militias come through looking for kids thirteen, fourteen, fifteen years old. When they find them it's off to the barracks, into uniforms, and out to the mountains to fight the guerrillas. They're cannon fodder, that's all."

Other things besides bullets can kill, of course, so there are poisons in the land of death to kill off the energy of youth. There was an incredible upswing in the use of alcohol and drugs, in prostitution, and in gambling about this time. During "mopping-up operations" the army never bothered with the drug addicts or alcoholics. They weren't dangerous, they were already dead. As for gambling, one colonel was heard to say, "We need more athletic fields. The boys are getting rebellious." Even recreation was used as a means of alienating youth.

• Religion itself, through the various new sects, entered the service of death. Soldiers were coerced into joining these sects. Small planes belonging to the new religions would fly over the cities with their "Jesus Saves" banners flying and their loudspeakers blaring, "This is a time of crisis! The devil is on the loose, threatening law and order!" The name of the game was "conversion," and if you "accepted Jesus" you were supposed to step outside with a little mirror and flash a signal up to the plane. A Puerto Rican evangelist was specially invited by José Napoleón Duarte to hold forth in the Flor Blanca Stadium every week. People would be transported to the stadium in trucks, and for hours on end the evangelist and his team would get them to shout, weep, and pray hysterically—and then he would drive out of them "the demons of Chalatenango and Morazán"—the popular militias.

Death in different masks, everywhere challenged our faith in the God of life.

The Shining Death of Father Rutilio

> *The twelfth of March.*
> *A machine-gun barks.*
> *The rich are happy.*
> *But the Padre still lives!*
>
> *Chabela remembers it,*
> *And Don Nicolás, too,*
> *And Don Pedro will fight for him*
> *And the people will march to battle.*
>
> *And if we must die in the struggle,*
> *Fighting with all our hearts,*
> *Though they kill us every one,*
> *Never shall we waver. . . .*
> —Battle Song in honor of Father Rutilio Grande,
> composed by the communities

Our incarnation in the persecuted people in this land of death challenged us to take up new tasks, new ways of being "doorkeepers." We knew our God was faithful to the hope of the poor. So we had to find a way to use this conviction, this hope, to overcome people's fear. The whole church, like Jesus in the country of Tyre and Sidon, was being importuned by a "Canaanite woman" to work some sign, to go beyond the confines of its "spiritual" concerns and pronounce some enlightening word in our tragic national situation.

One week after the fraudulent elections of February 1977 the hour of decision struck. In the Plaza de la Libertad in San Salvador, people were calling for honesty at the polls. They were massacred in the shrine of the Rosary. The popular organizations—the "foreigners, the "Canaanite woman"—rushed to tell Archbishop Romero. He had been archbishop of San Salvador for only five days. It was not easy for him to decide what to do. He had not yet been converted. Bishops Chávez and Rivera were the ones who reacted, and their intervention saved many a life, that day although many, too many, were killed.

The great "doorkeeper" in those days was Father Rutilio Grande. He it was who threw open the doors of hope to the whole country. Father Mario Bernal had just been expelled from the country and now it was Rutilio's prophetic voice that rang crisp and clear: "All we human beings have a common Father. That makes us all brothers and sisters. But some of our brothers and sisters are Cains. And in our country there are Cains who claim that God is on their side, and that's when things are really bad."

Rutilio Grande was the doorkeeper who called everyone to a communion of sisters and brothers in a land of Cains. Scarcely a month after he had pronounced his powerful words, the Cains killed him. His death opened Archbishop Romero's eyes to the reality of a martyred people, and turned him into a prophet of colossal stature. We who had known the old Bishop Romero were simply astounded. He was a new person. No miracle drove the community forward in its commitment as did the miracle of the conversion of their shepherd. And it was the blood of Rutilio that worked this miracle. Rutilio's was truly a shining death, and it nourished our hope that life would turn out to be stronger than anything else. With Archbishop Romero's conversion, the whole church in El Salvador, shepherd and flock together, began to be a doorkeeper, began to issue a constant call to live the gospel, to live hope in the land of death.

The Church Takes a Vow of Poverty

Poverty as an evangelical virtue is a protest against the tyranny of having, of possessing and of pure self-assertion. It impels those practicing it into practical solidarity with those poor whose poverty is not a matter of virtue but is their condition of life and the situation exacted of them by society.
—Johannes Metz, *Followers of Christ*

After Rutilio's murder, Archbishop Romero decided that he would "not take part in official ceremonies until the present situation is clarified." This decision led the whole church to take a new stance. Up until now, the church had occasionally criticized the power structure, it is true. But sometimes it seemed to be much too close to it.

The archbishop's absence from the inauguration of the new president, General Romero, was a serious indictment of the regime. It was a surprising action, and tremendously conscientizing.

Everything had changed. Archbishop Romero visited the communities, consulted and inquired what their criteria were for judging a situation and then acting. He stood firm: as long as the murder of Father Rutilio and his two peasant companions remained unexplained, until the exiled priests were permitted to return, until the cessation of repression of the people—the church would not dialogue with the government.

The *Pax Constantiniana* that had joined the spiritual and temporal powers together for centuries in El Salvador was broken. On July 1, 1977, the Salvadoran church made its solemn vow of poverty. Nor were consequences long in coming. The church in El Salvador began to lose and gain: it lost honor and reverence, and gained persecution, attacks, and slander.

The church's new solidarity with the poor of the whole country made the church recognizable once more as the protector of these poor. Now the poor saw in the church the face of Jesus, who scandalized the mighty, dined with sinners, and was always found on the side of the poor.

Everything changed. Two months after Rutilio's murder, another priest fell: Alfonso Navarro. The communities began to venerate these fallen as new martyrs, and we sang hope-filled songs of their resurrection. They had "gone ahead of us in faith," and were marking out a hard road indeed.

> Truth-telling's like a river
> Where freedom, once oppressed, flows again.
> But the bed is lined
> With blood-flowers, all living,
> The blood of people suffering,
> The blood of people crying.

Alfonso, Father Navarro,
Smashed lies your face
By bullet and club—
Open your veins,
By the thousands,
Sowing your words
Along the sidewalks of your people.
For you have risen!

The poverty of our church was being celebrated in the death of its priests, its catechists, its *campesinos*. Each day, for Archbishop Romero and every one of us, it was clearer that our church of poverty was under sentence to crucifixion and death, for it was following in the footsteps of Jesus.

The Church Takes a Vow of Purity

Celibacy as an evangelical virtue is the expression of an insatiable longing for the day of the Lord. It impels towards solidarity with those unmarried people whose celibacy (that is to say, loneliness; that is to say, not having anyone) is not a virtue but their social destiny, and towards those who are shut up in lack of expectation and in resignation.

—Johannes Metz, *Followers of Christ*

When Jesus expelled demons, he not only liberated individual persons, but also tore the mask from the face of the demons present in the sociopolitical system of his time. Our communities had discovered the connection between the two kinds of exorcism in daily practice. If it was necessary to liberate a brother from his alcoholism, it was just as necessary to deliver a society that provided no other escape from injustice but alcohol. So it was with all the other demons.

As repression intensified in El Salvador, it gradually became clear to us that our land was the victim of a truly demonic plan. The objective of this plan was to exterminate the people, if necessary, to maintain the system. When we saw Archbishop Romero fall, we understood how diabolical the imperialist designs on our country were. The imperialists would stop at nothing, would spare no one. The justification for everything was "communism." In the name of anticommunism, everything was permitted. All those murders were justified.

Archbishop Romero had become the great exorcist in our church. He battled the demon's plan, and he taught us all to drive the demon of fear from our own hearts. He fortified us in the same struggle that he was waging.

The murder of Father Ernesto Barrera on November 28, 1978, was a terribly difficult moment for the great exorcist Archbishop Romero. Here is how another priest, Ernesto's companion, tells the story.

Today at noon the news spread by word of mouth in the chancery corridors. "Neto's dead. He's been killed in a gun battle."

The first priest I saw shouted, "Now what?" Spelled out, his quick question meant: It was one thing when they got Rutilio and Alfonso, but this time the church is in big trouble. We've been harboring people like Neto, and he's turned out to be a "terrorist."

Suddenly the archbishop sent for all of us. He asked his perpetual question: "Tell me, what do you think we should do?" This man was feeling deep pain. A few months ago, he entrusted Neto and me with the assignment of seeing to a Christian presence in the union movement. And when people said we couldn't be trusted, he stood up for us, and especially for Neto.

It's hard to talk tonight. Most people were harsh. Marcos, for instance, said, "Give the family the body and let them bury him in their little village."

Everybody gave the Archbishop their views. When Jesús' turn came, he spoke very emotionally, and there were tears in his eyes. "Your Excellency, we're not sure how Neto died. But we know that if he died with a gun in his hand he wasn't just looking out for his own skin. He must have been acting out of faith in Christ and love for the people. He must have died fighting for the ideals of the poor, the, marginalized the exploited. He must have died defending the cause of the poor. I think the least we can do is to give him Christian burial and a priest's funeral.

When we were all finished, His Excellency surprised us with a question. His logic was different from ours. "Don't you think Neto's mother will be there with her son's body, without asking questions about his activities or his methods? Well, his bishop will have to be there too."

Archbishop Romero never learned how Neto died. The circumstances of his death were shrouded in meticulous governmental confusion. The official version spoke of a confrontation between the army and guerrillas. But the forensic pathologist sent by the archbishop reported that Neto's body showed signs of savage torture about the head and the face with a rifle butt and that there were electrical burns on other parts of his body. The only witness was captured by the security forces and later murdered. And so Archbishop Romero said: "We have evidence that Father Barrera did not die in an 'armed confrontation,' as the police have called it, but that he was first tortured and then shot to death at close range. I accuse the police of his murder."

The priest who had been Neto's companion in his work remarked, "Our bishop once again places himself in the human world of honesty and loyalty to his own option. He had taken Neto's side in life, and after the judgment he will be with him again."

In taking Neto's side that day in "getting its hands dirty," our church, in the person of Archbishop Romero, made its vow of purity. It accepted the curse of claiming the body of the accursed, one whose titles included "terrorist" and "communist." In making this choice, our church had made itself available to its people.

The love that was so active in our communities, yes, and the pastoral love of our priests, was being purified day by day in unconditional commitment to the poor. And in this consistent commitment the devil was driven out time and time again. The light was noonday-bright now, and the demon's machinations were rapidly exposed.

Our church was no longer the defender of impure interests. Now its love was free and freeing. We had a liberating church.

Illiterate No Longer

> *We are presently experiencing a grave economic and political crisis in our country. But there can be no doubt that our people have gradually become more conscientized and better organized. Thus they have begun to be capable of taking the future of El Salvador in hand. They alone will be able to manage the crisis.*
>
> *It would be unjust and deplorable were interference by foreign powers to frustrate the Salvadoran people, repress them, and present obstacles to their autonomous decision regarding the best economic and political path for our homeland to follow.*
>
> —Letter of Archbishop Romero
to President Jimmy Carter, Feb. 17, 1980

Those in our communities who were charged with the mission of being readers of reality, interpreters for their sisters and brothers of what was happening, now had great difficulty in carrying out their task. The Catholic radio station was dynamited. So was the Catholic weekly paper, *Orientación*. All of the independent newspapers were destroyed. The national university was bombed, as was the Catholic university's printing press.

But the people kept scrawling their slogans on the walls. They kept printing their flyers, in rectories now at the risk of their lives. Reading material was all under formal or informal censorship. The people's memory of the murdered priests was to be effaced. Even photos of the priest were not to be shown.

We met in secret. The children stood lookout while their elders "read"—reflected, in the light of faith, on what was occurring. Our lectors clarified, informed, pointed out directions. We felt compelled to analyze the pass to which things had come.

With the coup of October 1979 it finally became clear to everybody that our country was a target of imperialist strategy in Central America. The coup, the junta, the reforms—all of these things screamed at us from the housetops that we were being used. The popular organizations, now grown strong, denounced the outrage. "Words *no,* deeds *sí!*" was the motto at the rallies. But the deeds were those of a waxing oppression, the like of which had never been seen before. At the same time military and economic aid from the United States began to come in unprecedented amounts to shore up the government that that country had put in power as part of its strategy to curb the popular movement.

Archbishop Romero, the great reader of Salvadoran reality, refused to read daily life in abstract terms. His pronouncements were a powerful light shed on concrete reality. His letter to President Carter was an expression of his enormous capability as lector, as reader, in the Christian community.

In those days our communities used to show Father Peyton's films on the mysteries of the rosary. They helped us. The people identified the suffering Jesus with our oppressed, tortured, crucified people. And they identified Pilate with the criminal empire that had laid such a heavy cross on the shoulders of our people.

It was our readers' mission to keep the people's hope alive in the midst of such bitter suffering. The "readers" of the popular organizations did the same thing. And they made use of the churches. Wherever the good news of the gospel was preached, the good news of El Salvador's future liberation was proclaimed as well. In January 1980 Radio Venceremos—("We Shall Prevail")—was born.

One of the most important readings of reality done by the great lector Archbishop Romero about this time was contained in his Pastoral Letter "Church of the Poor and Popular Organizations," which he directed be read and reflected on in all the communities. He saw the importance of this subject in the current circumstances of national life.

At this same time, members of our communities, men and women of fine political talent, placed their gifts at the service of the popular organizations. Archbishop Romero did an excellent job of "reading" when he called the various organizations together in a dynamic unity. In our communities, this call was "transcendental": not all of our members were committed to the popular organizations. Coordinating committees were formed at the grassroots to overcome divisions among the organizations and battle the constant temptation to fanaticism (the temptation to "deify one's own organization," as the archbishop liked to put it).

This message on popular organization, on the unity of all of the organizations, and on the goal of an authentic popular program for the country was a constant theme of Archbishop Romero's preaching and therefore of reflection in our communities. His prophetic vision pointed us toward the future, and sowed seeds of hope in the land of death.

The Church Takes a Vow of Obedience

Obedience as an evangelical virtue is the radical and uncalculated surrender of one's life to God the Father who raises up and liberates. It impels one to stand close to those for whom obedience is not a matter of virtue but the sign of oppression and of being placed in tutelage, and to do this in a practical way. And if there is a growing proportion between the mystical and the political aspects of the radical nature of following Christ, then the more radical the manner in which this obedience is put into practice, the more uplifting and liberating but also unsettling the effect it has within the life of the individual, of the community and of the Church.

—Johannes Metz, *Followers of Christ*

Our readings of reality provoked questions, discoveries, and insecurities. We were adopting a stance of public disobedience to the regime. We had learned that it was illicit to obey unjust laws and an unjust sytem. It was God who was to be obeyed. A clear-cut division sprang into being in the bosom of the church. Not all of the bishops thought as Archbishop Romero. Conformism on the part of a large number of Christians led them to see our communities as a divisive factor in the church. How were we to find God's will in such confusion, in such contradictory positions? It was the hour of participation, and Christians involved in the popular organizations, in the political opposition, wanted to do their duty in the church as well. This would mean confrontation with bishops so different from Archbishop Romero.

We discovered what it means to obey. It means obeying God present in the signs of the times. It means being faithful to the preferential option for the poor. Only such fidelity, such loyalty, can open the way to the dynamic unity of the church. In Archbishop Romero's practice we saw that God is greater than the church. The church is the sacrament of God. But when the church fails in this sacramental mission, God is not reduced to the dimensions of the church. God keeps being God.

On March 23, 1980, the eve of his assassination, when Archbishop Romero publicly called on the soldiers to disobey the orders of their superiors, our church pronounced its solemn vow of obedience.

On the Wounds, Oil and Love

The disciple is not superior to his teacher, nor the slave to his master. It is enough for the disciple that he should grow to be like his teacher, and the slave like his master. If they have called the master of the house Beelzebul, what will they not say of his household?

Do not be afraid of them therefore. For everything that is now covered will be uncovered, and everything now hidden will be made clear. What I say to you in the dark, tell in the daylight; what you hear in whispers, proclaim from the housetops.

Do not be afraid of those who kill the body but cannot kill the soul: fear him rather who can destroy both body and soul in hell. Can you not buy two sparrows for a penny? And yet not one falls to the ground without your Father knowing. Why, every hair on your head has been counted. So there is no need to be afraid: you are worth more than hundreds of sparrows.

—Matthew 10:24–31

Repression was on the upsurge again. In a letter dated February 15, one of our priests wrote:

We're up to our neck in problems here. The popular organizations are more active than ever and repression has kept pace. A member of one of our Christian groups was kidnapped last Tuesday. He was a schoolteacher. We don't know where he is or what has happened to him, and we don't have much hope of seeing him again. Every day they uncover more corpses. Yesterday was the saddest day of my life. The teacher's students said they'd seen his body on the way into a village an hour from here. We went to see, along with his wife and some relatives. The village justice of the peace had processed ten bodies the day before. He said it happened every day. We were thinking that one of the ten, one who hadn't been identified, might be our friend. He was already buried, but we got permission to exhume him, so we got a pick and shovel and went to the cemetery. We dug up the body. It was miserably tortured. But it wasn't his. When we got back, we were told that they *had* found the body while we were gone. We went to look. We ran into a few people on a little bridge. They told us there were corpses every day. And yes, "This morning we buried a teacher." But the description didn't fit. Then, while we were there at the bridge, still another body turned up, this time along the river. Torture again. We rolled it over to look at its face. But it still wasn't our friend. This time his wife broke down. We're going to keep looking. We don't really have any hope of finding him, not alive anyway. Can God be indifferent to this much suffering?

In this way, by being so close to death, we discovered a new way of being "acolytes." "Acolyte" means "one who accompanies." This new way consisted in accompanying those who were suffering—being their companions along their way of the cross, their way of pain, and helping them not to be afraid. Some of the "acolytes" in our communities gave nursing and first-aid courses. We learned to give shots to relieve physical and mental pain. Our communities turned into walking hospitals. Dozens of first-aid kits were always ready to be rushed out to the wounded.

Another way of being an acolyte was to help take care of refugees fleeing the campaigns the army was mounting out in the countryside. These campaigns were really criminal. The refugees would come to the capital. Women and old people would arrive with a bundle of clothes and a bunch of crying kids. They would come to the archbishop's house and ask for help. The stories they told were simply horrible. So the church opened its doors and started setting up emergency aid.

Being an acolyte meant risking your life. There was the day when a youth was shot fifty yards from the parish center. One of our acolytes ran up to help him. Suddenly he felt the barrel of a rifle in his shoulder. "Are you a relative?"

"No," came the quick reply, "but he's a human being, and he needs treatment."

"Get lost, unless you're lookin' to get the same."

Up rolled an army truck. They gave the boy the coup de grâce and dragged his body toward the truck, hauling it by the hair leaving a bloody trail across the street. They threw it into the truck on top of other bodies and drove away.

One day I went to the International Red Cross to get help. I tried to set something up with them to take care of the wounded. They couldn't help. They were forced to hand over the wounded to the security forces, who would later kill them.

There was the same risk of death for acolytes who encouraged our people along the road by reminding them that today's pain was tomorrow's redemption. Father Alirio Napoleón Macías, of the diocese of San Vincente, had denounced the arbitrary searches, the death squads, the kidnappings. They killed him in his church, San Esteban in Catarina, in August 1979, as he was leaving the sacristy for the altar.

> New Calvary, Catarina,
> The place where a cross stands high
> Over Padre Macías,
> Who followed Jesus to die.

Many were the fallen, then—fallen in the service of healing the wounds of the people in the trenches of unselfish service—in the footsteps of Jesus, the Man of Sorrows.

Sorrow, Despair, Violence

They came to a small estate called Gethsemane, and Jesus said to his disciples, "Stay here while I pray." Then he took Peter and James and John with him. And a sudden fear came over him, and great distress. And he said to them, "My soul is sorrowful to the point of death. Wait here, and keep awake." And going on a little further he threw himself on the ground and prayed that, if it were possible, this hour might pass him by. "Abba (Father)!" he said. "Everything is possible for you. Take this cup away from me. But let it be as you, not I, would have it."

—Mark 14:32-36

We became familiar with the temptation of sorrow, as Jesus did in Gethsemane. I can still hear Silvia: "I'm just in agony. Sometimes I think it would have been better not to preach the gospel. If people's consciousness hadn't been raised at least they wouldn't have died. I feel sad, I feel deathly sad, when I think of all we've done, and how many people committed themselves, and now they've been killed. . . ." She needed comfort and counsel in that hour of deep sorrow.

And in that same hour, with death part of the daily routine, many of us could no longer bear up under the tension, and "fell asleep," like Peter, James, and John in Gethsemane.

To overcome this temptation, we had to pray, fast, and watch. We spent whole days keeping vigil in the cathedral, or in the Church of the Holy Rosary. Our vigils were a call to the Christians of the whole world to stay awake with us and not permit the genocide of the Salvadoran people.

We came to understand that, in that historic hour, El Salvador was the Suffering Servant of Yahweh for all the nations. We were a challenge to the hope of all peoples: a small, poor country was facing up to the most powerful empire on earth. We understood that in our struggle all the poor of the earth were struggling too. And the responsibility of the undertaking was so great that we were constantly immersed in a vast temptation to . . . stumble, to back down, to give up in despair.

We discovered that our hour of pain was the world's salvation. Of course that didn't stop the pain. And the cruelty was increasing constantly. Now it was war—open war—between the popular forces and the official army. Genocide, North American intervention, and the limitless heroism of our people grew apace.

Violence had been an occasional theme of our reflections for a good while. Now we meditated and discussed it constantly.

Yes, nonviolence had always been our ideal, but an ideal we aimed at. Salvadoran reality was so far from this ideal that nonviolence alone was not enough—not even in the name of the gospel. We just couldn't bring ourselves to use "nonviolence" as an alibi that would actually make us the accomplices of a special type of criminal: those who preach nonviolence while practicing the most extreme violence with their arms race, their economic exploitation, and their institutionalized injustice. Our violence was so very clearly a defensive violence, a violence forced on us by constant, unremitting violence, that to deny its legitimacy in the name of the gospel would have been to deny the gospel. Recent history in El Salvador had proved that all peaceful "solutions"—protests, reformist laws, elections, just demands—all these ways had been closed off, violently.

We opened the gospel and we read, "If anyone hits you on the right cheek, offer him the other as well" (Mt 5:39). We came to understand that this counsel carries no weight when it is the torturer who utters it. It is a counsel from the lips of Jesus, not from his attackers. The forces of death may not be allowed to use these words for their own purposes. They may not be allowed to use them to challenge us to passivity.

We meditated on "You shall not kill." We read this commandment of God in the Salvadoran situation, and saw that it did not mean "You shall not defend yourselves," but, "You shall not allow people to kill people." This commandment was given to us not to keep us from acting, but move us to action, to move us to participation. The ultimate, definitive question in El Salvador was: Which side are we on?

Not that the question of violence was an easy one. Submerged as we were in a world of violence, we sometimes experienced the temptation to respond with disproportionate, or unnecessary, violence, and Archbishop Romero warned us against this. Neither "mystical extreme" was in order—neither extreme violence nor extreme passivity. And this is what we prayed about.

Many priests had to leave the country at that time. They would have been killed otherwise. What happened in Gethsemane when the soldiers came looking for Jesus happened in our case too. "If I am the one you are looking for," Jesus told the soldiers, "let these others go" (Jn 18:8). Because we were with the poor, we were persecuted along with them. And for each of us there came the moment when the danger of losing our lives was imminent. So

Archbishop Romero and the community itself ordered us to leave. "Better to cry because you're leaving than because you're dead," they told me. And like the disciples, we fled. We fled to save our lives in obedience to the word of the people, which was the same as the word of Jesus: Here I am, these others can go. But Jesus was taken away. And the Salvadoran people, too, now started their real way of the cross, for now they were subjected to more violent repression than ever before. Jesus was being crucified again.

New Deaconships for a Country at War

See, my servant will prosper,
he shall be lifted up, exalted, rise to great heights.

As the crowds were appalled on seeing him
—so disfigured did he look
that he seemed no longer human—
so will the crowds be astonished at him,
and kings stand speechless before him;
for they shall see something never told
and witness something never heard before:
"Who could believe what we have heard,
and to whom has the power of Yahweh been revealed"?

Like a sapling he grew up in front of us,
like a root in arid ground.
Without beauty, without majesty (we saw him),
no looks to attract our eyes;
a thing despised and rejected by men,
a man of sorrows and familiar with suffering,
a man to make people screen their faces;
he was despised and we took no account of him.

And yet ours were the sufferings he bore,
ours the sorrows he carried.
But we, we thought of him as someone punished,
struck by God, and brought low.
Yet he was pierced through for our faults,
crushed for our sins.

> *On him lies a punishment that brings us peace,*
> *and through his wounds we are healed.*
>   —Isaiah 52:13–53:5

The service of the Salvadoran people on their way of the cross gave birth to new forms of deaconship in our church. The first new service was simply attempting to hold the communities together. The repression caused them terrible damage. Priests, nuns, catechists, directors were all victims of death and threats of death. Brave community members had gone off to full-time involvement in popular organizations, and were no longer constantly with us. The division within the church increased the fear and confusion of many of us. Many communities were without a priest, and felt at sea if their bishops took no care of them whatever in their hour of the cross.

This situation gave rise to the first efforts at intercommunity coordination. Without this coordination, we could see, the communities were doomed to disappear, to be destroyed. This crucial need for unity occasioned the creation of the National Coordinating Committee of the Popular Church of El Salvador. The purpose of this committee was to orient as many Christians as possible along the line of pastoral activity initiated by Archbishop Romero: pastoral activity that would be liberating for the masses, pastoral activity that would allow the communities to become a sign, pastoral activity that would provide support for committed Christians in the popular organizations. And so our coordinating committee originated as a genuine deaconship on behalf of our communities.

The war made for a massive displacement of the *campesino* population to urban areas. The elderly, women, and children were fleeing army operations and indiscriminate bombing for the capital. The war also sent a wave of refugees to the neighboring countries of Central America. These refugees and exiles had lost everything—their homes, their meager livestock, their hand tools. All they had left were their tears. Caring for these refugees became a deaconship for the whole church. Material and moral assistance to those fleeing oppression and death became a priority service. Not only pastoral centers, but even contemplative monasteries and convents opened their doors. The communities set up every kind of assistance program. And the Eucharist became a very special sign and pledge of hope in every place where the refugees found asylum. Out beyond the borders of El Salvador, the Salvadoran church too was in exile in the Salvadorans who now must live their faith in sorrow in a foreign land.

The war raised new questions in our communities. Why should we not go out to where the popular army was in control? There too Christ should be proclaimed, should he not? There too hope in a new heaven and a new earth should be kept alive. There too we would surely find wounded to treat, children to teach, and a whole people with whom to celebrate the faith we all held in common. There the popular army was battling for the rights of God's people, and the Ark of the Covenant should go with them.

How well I remember our meditations on all these matters. How we asked God to help us find the answers! Which of us should be the deacons in the front lines? We would call them the Cyreneans. I remember shaking hands with Rogelio the night he went off to Morazán to be the Cyrenean there, hugging Silvia when she and her little team decided to go and be with Mary at the foot of the cross, go where they could feel God calling them. Those were grand, unforgettable moments.

From those trenches of hope, Rogelio wrote us many letters. We read them in our communities, with all the excitement of the Christians of two thousand years ago in Galatia, Corinth, and Thessalonika reading the letters of Paul. Here is one of Rogelio's letters.

Dear Brothers and Sisters,

Things are tough. I have to come to you for help. For eighteen days we've been surrounded by over a thousand soldiers. From the first day they've been attacking our territory tirelessly, day and night. They've destroyed everything they could, but they haven't been able to get into this liberated territory. The day we celebrated Archbishop Romero's anniversary they started bombing and strafing. We can't help thinking of what the Vietnamese people went through. In spite of everything, though, our region is holding out because our army is getting all kinds of help from the civilian population. We thank God. God's help is everywhere. We thank God for the readiness and the bravery of our fighters. Before attacking us the soldiers attacked the civilian population in the Junquillo. They killed old people, pregnant women, and children. I guess it wasn't enough to rob them of the little they had. The last attacks, with artillery fire and napalm bombardments, made me just as mad as hell. They seem to consider us wild beasts, and they have to hunt us till they catch us. They can't let us get away because we're so bad for the country. Unbelievable.

I love the people here. They're deeply religious people, men and women with hearts of gold, marvelously ready for the great commitment. Their faith has made them ready for anything. And now what can they do but go to war? There's no other way to get justice.

Our church has done a great job of conscientization here. It's been a prophetic church, there's no question about it, and that's a source of pride and satisfaction. This is what we've worked for. And of course we'll keep working. I think we have a great responsibility before the world. The world has a lot of confidence in us. We've got a lot of credibility in its eyes. We have moral authority.

So from Morazán I beg you: don't let up on your peace efforts. And remember: peace will be authentic only if it respects our people. Specifically: (1) please explain our people's struggle for justice in every way that you can; (2) don't let the government junta get away with a masquerade like this; (3) denounce the North American intervention—they're trying to destroy the hopes of our people; (4) keep encouraging the popular movement.

These are things that people can do only if they've taken sides with the poor. What other choice do we have if we don't want to be traitors to our faith? In Puebla our church made a "preferential option for the poor." All of us, bishops, priests, religious, and lay persons, have to accept our historical responsibility. All of us must cooperate in the liberation of our people. This is how we must witness to our living God.

Last, I want to tell you how happy I am to be here. Now I'm physically cooperating in our liberation. Now I'm practicing what I've been preaching! My commitment is respected by guerilla leaders and population alike. I've never felt so much a priest. And I've never felt so united with you. We're one, you and I, in the love God has for us, and in the love we have for the poor—in whom God is revealed. Brothers and sisters, God expects a great deal of you now.

In union with you in Christ Jesus,
Rogelio

All of these new services—and especially their daily way of the cross, their pain, their wounds—made the Salvadoran people a servant people, a "deacon people" for all the peoples of the earth.

El Salvador at war is a diaconate. It is rendering a unique service to the universal church, a service that will hurry its conversion. Before the eyes of all the world, the boundless cruelty suffered by our people has a purpose: that all persons may acknowledge their sins. If we can grasp the drama of the Salvadoran people, we can recognize our faults and acknowledge our responsibilities in this drama. For the drama of the Salvadoran people is also a universal drama, in which a few have everything while everyone else lacks even a minimally decent human life. The drama of El Salvador is an outcry, a cry to the Western world, the democratic world, the Christian world, to be converted and live. A call to conversion is a precious service.

Three Moments in Holy Week

Then the chief priests and Pharisees called a meeting. "Here is this man working all these signs," they said, "and what action are we taking? If we let him go on in this way everybody will believe in him, and the Romans will come and destroy the Holy Place and our nation." One of them, Caiaphas, the high priest that year, said, "You don't seem to have grasped the situation at all; you fail to see that it is better for one man to die for the people, than for the whole nation to be destroyed.

—John 11:47–50

The Salvadoran people were becoming a priestly people. The doorkeepers, exorcists, readers, acolytes, and deacons of our communities were becoming priests, other Christs, by blood and persecution. In fact, the whole church in El Salvador was becoming a prophetic, priestly church.

How many times we relived, in our flesh and history, the passion of our elder brother Jesus! There have been three moments especially that for me were like moments in Holy Week.

January 22, 1980. Despite so many differences, the popular organizations had joined forces and had set up the Revolutionary Coordinating Committee of the Masses. This new oneness was a sign of the liberation to come, and so it was celebrated in the streets in the most gigantic rally El Salvador had ever seen. Jesus, who died "that they may be one," made his triumphal entry into Jerusalem on this day. This is how we saw it and felt it. His entry was simple, poor, and humble. On a donkey, you might say. The only "triumphal entries" we had ever seen had been the big, showy parades when the military flaunted all its war material—big "rallies" celebrating violence and oppression, and all the people were expected to cheer the empty, foolish speeches.

But today was different. This was truly Hosanna Sunday in El Salvador. This was the advance celebration of the liberation. This new popular oneness could mean only one thing: we were going to win. And so the young and the poor—in other words, the ever-downtrodden—took over the streets. This was popular triumph.

Triumph, yes, but triumphalism it was surely not. In our very joy, we found the cross. Poison rained down from the sky. Bullets ricocheted in the corners. Many, many people were killed or wounded. And yet, in spite of all their suffering, the priestly people of El Salvador grasped that this was their Palm Sunday celebration.

January 20, 1979, was Holy Thursday for our church. Father Octavio Ortiz was meeting with some young people in the parish hall of Saint Anthony Abbott. Octavio was a simple man, a *campesino,* who had long devoted his life to our communities. He had already had much experience in "giving his life." Octavio's presence was like the life-giving rain that falls on a field of new corn. The evening before, he had reflected with the young people on Jesus' healing of the blind. (Jesus came to give sight to the blind. Now, who are the blind of El Salvador?) And in the dawn light of the twentieth, an army death squad marched in and murdered four youths and Octavio.

Octavio had had his first pastoral experience in the slums, with us. He had been ordained a priest in our community and had celebrated his first Mass with us. He was our great friend. We all felt close to him. And now he was celebrating his last Eucharist, his Last Supper. His blood mixed with the blood of his young friends and the blood of the whole people in the greatest offering he could give to God, the greatest proof of his love. This was not lost on the people who loved him. Soon they were singing, in the Eucharist:

What a strange new morning!
It was not the sun
Beyond the mountain,
But the shining example of someone brave we knew—
Someone who gave his innocent soul for the oppressed,
And his life for his friends,
That we, the blind, might see.
Father Octavio has left this land,
Crushed by the fierce and the mighty,
Like the prophets who go to heaven,
As the poet sang.
And this is our hope:
That this blood win him glory!
For he has opened a new history:
The history of the New Person.

Octavio's blood taught us that the Eucharist must be celebrated in life itself, and that its sacramental celebration has meaning only if those who share in it are giving the gift of their lives.

A hundred priests celebrated Octavio's funeral in the cathedral. The people rose to applaud him as his corpse was borne past them. And in their determination to go on with their struggle—which is what all this applause meant, we knew—we understood it would be Easter in El Salvador any moment now, and that today's Holy Thursday was the celebration of a fertile, life-giving sacrifice.

Our people had first gotten up and walked. Then they had been ordained a eucharistic people. Now they had a voice. The steady, untiring voice of their archbishop had given them back their own voice. And so he must die. By murdering Archbishop Romero, on March 24, 1979, the killers thought that they could stifle the voice of the people. The army chiefs of staff decreed that the archbishop was a "communist subversive." The United States government decreed that he was an "agitator," a disturber of the democratic order and the national security. The Salvadoran government junta decreed that he was a dangerous anti-patriot. And so he was murdered, while celebrating Mass, with a single bullet through the heart.

In the assassination of our archbishop we have a kind of symbol and image of the genocide of the Salvadoran people. Through that open heart passed the judgment of the world and the "sin of the world." Now Oscar Arnulfo Romero is a shining signal to the church universal in these times of struggle and hope. In our archbishop, God has taken sides with the poor in history, has taken up the cause of the peoples who go in quest of their liberation, has taken up the cause of the church that has committed itself to their struggle. Since the death of the shepherd every day is Good Friday for the flock, this people of priests, with blood on their vestments every day of the year, offer up to God a pleasing sacrifice for the world's redemption.

This is our hope.

I finish this book more than a year after Archbishop Romero's assassination. It is still Good Friday in El Salvador. Yet a little while, and we shall hear the end of the story: resurrection, the Salvadoran people's Easter, and an empty tomb in the midst of our communities. The glory of that day of peace has yet to dawn. But this is our hope: as Jesus, who was crucified, was raised by God, this crucified people too will rise. Indeed, it is rising even as I write these lines.

Archbishop Romero Pastoral Center

By Ignacio Ellacuría, S.J.
and Jon Sobrino, S.J.

The church of El Salvador, the church of Latin America, and the church universal possess a permanent source of inspiration and Christian encouragement in Archbishop Oscar Arnulfo Romero. This inspiration and encouragement ought surely to be preserved and fostered. Pope John Paul II prayed at Archbishop Romero's tomb and called him a "zealous, venerated pastor." Archbishop Rivera y Damas of San Salvador has called him a "martyr of our own times." Archbishop Romero is a model and inspiration for so many, in their spiritual life, in their pastoral activity, in their commitment to the very poorest and neediest, and in their theological reflection. For the poor of El Salvador and many other countries, Archbishop Romero is the mainstay of faith and hope. The people remember him as their voice and their advocate.

In order to keep Archbishop Romero's memory alive and operative, to keep his presence effective, the Society of Jesus has established a "pastoral center" dedicated to that memory. This center consists of a chapel and an area for theological reflection. It stands at the edge of the campus of Central American University, the Jesuit university of El Salvador. Our Pastoral Center is not only home base for a pastoral, liturgical, and theological apostolate to the university's six thousand students, but is placed in the service of the whole people of God, as an instrument for their theological enlightenment and "pastoral accompaniment."

The specific purpose of the Center for Theological Reflection is to promote and coordinate theological and pastoral work already being waged by the Jesuits. Among the more theological of these activities are the publication of the *Revista Latinoamericana de Teología*, a theological journal whose first issue appeared in April 1984; the series of monographs, *Teología Latinoamericana*; and a course of studies for the degree of master of sacred theology. Among our more pastoral activities are the publication of the bi-weekly newsletter *Carta a las Iglesias* ("Letter to the Churches"); the series of volumes entitled *La Iglesia en América Latina*; and "Ciencias Religiosas y Morales," a three-year program geared to the needs of lay pastoral ministers and community leaders.

The purpose of these projects, as well as of others such as Christian training pamphlets, retreats for farmers and students, or talks and workshops, is to provide theological enlightenment and a pastoral "accompaniment" for the church on its journey, a theological and pastoral service to a people of the poor along the pathways of their concrete sufferings and hopes. Accordingly, the theology to be developed must be one capable of enlightening the whole people of God; the pastoral approach must be calculated to address the concrete sufferings and hopes of the people themselves, and to provide them with an opportunity for self-expression.

The Pastoral Center welcomes all who are interested in promoting the reign of God in El Salvador. It seeks to make its resources and staff available to the Christian religious individuals and groups, Catholic and non-Catholic, who are such frequent visitors to our country. It means to be at the service especially of those who enlighten the pathways of God's people through a theological or pastoral ministry. It makes its facilities available for courses of study, reflection, and community meetings.

We wish to dedicate these activities to the memory of Archbishop Romero because they are guided by his spirit. As this Pastoral Center symbolizes Archbishop Romero's universal inspiration, we intend to seek out as universal a support for it as possible. Our hope is that such support would be forthcoming from all continents and from most of the churches, to celebrate the memory of Archbishop Romero as well as to extend awareness of his spirit and his deeds.

Our aim is not great material achievement. This would not be according to the mind of Archbishop Romero. Our aim is to move out from a slim material basis to accomplish something worthwhile along the lines of a preferential option for the poor—something which will redound to the increase of faith, hope, justice, and love in our people and in the people of God throughout the world. In our concrete situation, of course, this means working for peace and justice. Our hope is to be able to bring to as full a fruition as possible the seeds that Archbishop Romero planted in such fine soil by his blood and his word. All who desire to join us in this endeavor are cordially invited to do so in the way and to the extent that they will deem suitable.

Contributions have already begun to arrive, and in a form that Archbishop Romero would certainly appreciate. Germany's Adveniat and the Society of Jesus have made sizable contributions, as have religious communities, agencies, bishops and priests in Europe, the United States, Canada, and Latin America. Most wonderfully, we have also received small contributions, sometimes in pennies, from communities of peasants, native Americans, and refugees. The soldiarity and love that come with these modest contributions make them great amounts indeed in the eyes of God. They inspire us to move ahead with this project; they prevent us from ever forgetting our purpose.

For more information on how to support the Archbishop Romero Pastoral Center, please write: Ignacio Ellacuría, Apartado (01) 168, San Salvador, El Salvador, C.A.